T0288266

CONCISE
LINCOLN
LIBRARY

—

EDITED BY RICHARD W. ETULAIN,
SARA VAUGHN GABBARD, AND
SYLVIA FRANK RODRIGUE

WILLIAM C. HARRIS

Lincoln and the Union Governors

Southern Illinois University Press
Carbondale

16 15 14 13   4 3 2 1

The Concise Lincoln Library has been made possible
in part through a generous donation by the Leland E.
and LaRita R. Boren Trust.

Library of Congress Cataloging-in-Publication Data
Harris, William C. (William Charles), 1933–
Lincoln and the Union Governors / William C. Harris.
pages cm. — (Concise Lincoln library)
Includes bibliographical references and index.
ISBN 978-0-8093-3288-5 (cloth : alk. paper)
ISBN 0-8093-3288-4 (cloth : alk. paper)
ISBN 978-0-8093-3289-2 (ebook)
ISBN 0-8093-3289-2 (ebook)
1. Lincoln, Abraham, 1809–1865—Relations with gover-
nors. 2. United States—History—Civil War, 1861–1865
—Political aspects. 3. United States—Politics and
government—1861–1865. 4. Governors—United States
—History—19th century. I. Title.
E457.2.H336 2013
973.7092—dc23   2013010556

Printed on recycled paper. ♻
The paper used in this publication meets the mini-
mum requirements of American National Standard
for Information Sciences—Petrmanence of Paper for
Printed Library Materials, ANSI Z39.48-1992. ∞

For the "Dinosaur Diners," who, usually with good humor, tolerated my Lincoln stories

CONTENTS

Gallery of illustrations following page 78

LINCOLN AND THE UNION GOVERNORS

INTRODUCTION

Modern historians and students of the Civil War have not given proper credit to the contribution that the Union governors made in winning the war and preserving the nation. The relationship of these state executives with Lincoln, while sometimes difficult, was essential to the Union's success. Lincoln recognized that in dealing with the governors and securing their cooperation in the war, he had to tread carefully and, unless necessary to prevent the obstruction of the war effort, avoid violating their constitutional authority under the federal system of government. The Union governors, though usually not as extreme as their Confederate counterparts, sought to uphold states' rights, or what some called state "sovereignty."

Fortunately for Lincoln and the war effort, the Northern governors, except for Horatio Seymour of New York and Joel Parker of New Jersey, both elected in 1862, belonged to Lincoln's Union or Republican Party coalition and supported the president's war policies. Seymour and Parker, though a thorn in Lincoln's side, remained true to the Union. In the Far West, the governors of California and Oregon from 1861 until 1862 were Democrats who supported the Union, though grudgingly in the case of John Whiteaker of Oregon. The border slave state governors, except for Claiborne Fox Jackson of Missouri, were loyal but did not affiliate with Lincoln's party. Jackson fled south in July 1861, leaving a Union provisional government in control of the state. In 1865, Thomas Fletcher of Missouri became the first Republican governor of a border state.

Lincoln, then and later, has been accused of seeking to diminish the power of the states and the governors during the war. His purpose, critics have charged, was to create a strong or "consolidated" government in Washington for the fulfillment of what they perceived as the national doctrine of Lincoln's old Whig Party. In an influential essay, Edmund Wilson, a popular American man of letters, compared Lincoln to Bismarck and Lenin as a ruthless creator of national unity.[1] Historian Morton Keller has rightly said that "this view ignores the context of cultural and institutional restraints in which a mid-nineteenth century American President worked." Keller could have added that the political context also inhibited the president's actions had he wanted to centralize his authority. Lincoln's achievement, Keller writes, "was not so much to resolve the conflict between localism and centralism as to keep that conflict from fatally crippling the war effort."[2]

Government activity, particularly in military matters and on constitutional issues, surged at all levels of government during the war. This should not suggest, however, that Lincoln sought to make federal expansion and presidential power permanent features of the government. Still, it was virtually inevitable that after the war, the size of the government would not be reduced to its antebellum level as preferred by the Democrats. In his relations with the governors, Lincoln's purpose was to gain and retain their assistance in suppressing the rebellion and eventually in ending slavery. He did not conceive of the establishment of a "consolidated government" in Washington at the expense of state authority. Lincoln understood clearly that the war was a "people's war," necessitating the active support of local and state authorities.

Neither Lincoln nor the governors, in their relationships with each other and in their management of affairs, were free of mistakes or differences. The unprecedented military demands to fight a national war for survival; the traditional role of the governors in controlling and providing for state troops; the technical problems of communications inherent in such a large country; the decentralized political structure of the country, with frequent state and local elections; and the uncertainties and passions generated by the war made conflict between Washington and the state capitals inevitable. The governors at times complained to Lincoln about his inaction and lack of firmness and also about the War Department and the commanding generals' incompetence. However, they usually cooperated with him, even on controversial issues like military conscription and emancipation, which bitterly divided the people of their states. The governors were often ahead of Lincoln in raising troops, providing for their needs and those of their families, and suppressing "traitors" at home. Governors Oliver P. Morton of Indiana; David Tod, a former Democrat, of Ohio; Richard Yates of Illinois; Samuel J. Kirkwood of Iowa; Andrew G. Curtin of Pennsylvania; Edwin D. Morgan of New York, Seymour's predecessor; and John A. Andrew of Massachusetts were virtually "war ministers," especially in 1861 to 1862.

The purpose of this book is to provide the general reading public with an understanding of the role of the governors and their relationship with Lincoln in achieving Union victory and emancipation. The book also is designed to provide insights into Lincoln's management of the daunting and complex issues involved in securing and maintaining support for the war and his policies.

THE SECESSION CRISIS

During the course of the Civil War, fifty-nine men served as governors of the twenty-five Union states. These included the governors of the Northern free states; West Virginia, which was admitted to statehood in 1863; Nevada, admitted in 1864; and the slave states of Delaware, Maryland, Kentucky, and Missouri, which remained faithful to the Union. They did not include the western territorial governors or those of the six rebel states—Virginia, Tennessee, Louisiana, Arkansas, North Carolina, and Texas—where Lincoln attempted to establish loyal governments, with mixed results. Of the fifty-nine, only Oliver P. Morton of Indiana, Andrew G. Curtin of Pennsylvania, William A. Buckingham of Connecticut, and John A. Andrew of Massachusetts served from the beginning of the war to the end. Richard Yates of Illinois and Austin Blair of Michigan held the office for almost all of the war.

Politically, the majority of the Northern governors, like Lincoln, became Republicans after a long affiliation with the prewar Whig Party. At least one of them, Alexander W. Randall of Wisconsin, had been both a Whig and a Democrat before affiliating with the antislavery Republican Party in the mid-1850s. Most of the border state governors also had associated with the Union Whig Party or its offshoot in the 1850s, the Know-Nothing Party, making it relatively easy for them to cooperate with Lincoln in preserving the Union, but not in his antislavery policies and military intervention in their states.

The governors often reflected different regional interests. The north-eastern governors were keenly attuned to the commercial, banking, and industrial interests of the East. Their counterparts in the West (today's Midwest) dutifully represented their section's agricultural concerns and dependence on the Mississippi-Ohio river system for the region's markets. The governors of the semi-frontier states of Minnesota, Iowa, Kansas, and Wisconsin, while vigorously supporting the war, were deeply concerned with Indian conflict, federal land policy, and railroad development. The new state of Kansas also faced the continuation of a bitter border struggle with proslavery elements in Missouri.

In the Far West, the governors of California and Oregon were concerned with political conflict at home and insecurity from In-dian attacks after the withdrawal of U.S. Army troops from frontier fortifications, especially in Oregon and the Washington territory. A conspiracy to establish a so-called "Pacific Republic," though exagger-ated, convulsed the Far West during the early part of the Civil War. Even after Republican governors replaced Southern rights' Democrats in 1862, California and Oregon still faced some of the same issues as their counterparts in the East, namely Lincoln's antislavery policies, his suspension of the writ of habeas corpus, and the Copperhead or antiwar threat.[1]

The Union governors of the border slave states had two over-whelming concerns in the war. They were determined to protect slavery, at least until 1863, and they were equally determined for their states to control race relations. They expected Lincoln to stand by his promise not to interfere with slavery in their states. In 1861, these governors also wanted to avoid being drawn into the middle of an internecine conflict between the North and the South, which they re-alized would be destructive and would tear their communities apart.

The Northern governors during the first part of the war acknowl-edged that slavery was wrong, but they held different views on what should or could be done about it. However, they agreed with Lincoln and with the Republican platform that slavery should not be permit-ted to expand into the western territories. While believing that slavery was the cause of the war, lower North governors often denounced the abolitionists as well as the Southern fire-eaters for the sectional division. The border state governors, on the other hand, placed the blame for the conflict almost squarely on the Northern antislavery agitators and the Republicans. Upper North governors, unlike their lower North counterparts, opposed the enforcement of the federal Fugitive Slave Act of 1850 for the return of escaping slaves to their masters. The New England governors and Austin Blair of Michigan, a native of upstate New York, were more ardent opponents of slavery and Southern society than their lower North colleagues. Still, at the beginning of the war, these governors largely muted their strong antislavery and anti-Southern opinions in order to secure a united North behind the war whose purpose, as announced by Lincoln, was to preserve the Union and its republican institutions. Furthermore, they did not desire to provoke the border states into secession by raising the specter of abolition in the South.

Even Governor John A. Andrew of Massachusetts, a staunch opponent of slavery, in 1861 sought to deflect the criticism of his antislavery friends who wanted him to demand the eradication of slavery as a war aim. Soon after Fort Sumter, he told the Massachusetts legislature that the top priority in the war must be to build up a strong Union sentiment in all of the states, including those on the border. "This is no war of sections," he exclaimed, "no war of North on South. . . . It is the struggle of the People to vindicate their own rights, to retain and invigorate the institutions of their fathers." Yet, Andrew admitted, "I do not forget . . . that 'subtle poison' [slavery] which has lurked always in our national system."[2] He repeated this message to a group of prominent citizens and merchants in New York on September 5. On this occasion, however, he avoided mentioning the "subtle poison" of slavery, though he announced that the war was also fought for "the rights of universal humanity." By the end of 1861, the Massachusetts governor had rejected Lincoln's conservative policy regarding slavery. He then joined emancipation to the primary national purpose of saving the Union. He did not believe that the two war aims were mutually exclusive. Andrew and his fellow upper North governors supported their states' personal liberty laws designed to protect fugitive slaves, despite pressure from the lower North and the border states to have these statutes repealed.[3]

Edwin D. Morgan of New York, Andrew G. Curtin of Pennsylvania, and Charles S. Olden of New Jersey, reflecting the majority opinion in their states, treaded even more softly on the slavery issue in 1861–62. Both Morgan and Curtin were Republicans; Olden was a Union Democrat. Although they were mildly antislavery, these governors focused on the suppression of the rebellion as the Union's sole purpose. They took their cue from Lincoln's inaugural address on March 4, 1861, and vehemently argued their position from the standpoint of republican ideology and the tremendous importance of sustaining the government. At the same time, the border slave state governors, while remaining loyal, repeatedly warned Lincoln and Congress in 1861–62 that their states would leave the Union if dominant Northern Republicans took action against slavery in the South. Over time, however, their opposition to emancipation as a war measure declined, though rarely out of any antislavery conviction.

The western governors generally supported the relatively conservative antislavery position favored by Lincoln. Their views, however, became more antislavery as the war became long and with no victory in sight. In January 1862, Governor Samuel J. Kirkwood of Iowa told his legislature, "The war is waged by our Government for the preservation of the Union, and not for the extinction of Slavery, unless the preservation of the one shall require the extinction of the other." The Iowa governor contended that "the friends of Slavery have in its supposed interest thrust this war with all its evils upon the country, and upon them and upon [slavery] be consequences." But Kirkwood assured the legislature that, if the war ended tomorrow with the preservation of the Union, "I would not now spend further treasure or further life to effect the extinction of Slavery." He would regret, however, that slavery had been left "to be our bane and pest in the future as in the past."[4] Governor Alexander Ramsey, in his message to the Minnesota legislature on March 6, 1862, announced that the people of the state were in favor of a vigorous prosecution of the war, but they opposed "our Senators and Representatives in Congress advocating the abolition of slavery . . . or any other unconstitutional measures."[5] Both Kirkwood and Ramsey later favored emancipation, and after the war, as a U.S. senator, Ramsey voted for the Reconstruction laws providing for black male suffrage in the former rebel states.

Only a few governors had met Lincoln before he traveled to Washington in February 1861 to assume office. One was Governor Andrew of Massachusetts, who, as a member of the Republican national committee to inform the president-elect officially of his nomination, had visited Lincoln in Springfield in May 1860. After his return to Boston, Andrew waxed effusive in his praise of the party's candidate. He told a Faneuil Hall audience that in listening to Lincoln, his "eyes were never visited with the vision of a human face, in which more transparent honesty and more benignant kindness were combined with more of the intellect and firmness which belong to masculine humanity."[6] During the war, however, Andrew found Lincoln wanting in the essential qualities of leadership—namely, firmness and a compelling commitment to the antislavery cause.

In early January 1861, Governor Kirkwood of Iowa, never having met Lincoln and wanting to sound him out on his policy toward secession, paid a surprise visit to Springfield. Kirkwood, a "plainly dressed and unobtrusive" farmer, met the president-elect in a local hotel room. The Iowa governor, a native of a border slave state, Maryland, later wrote that Lincoln "spoke calmly, earnestly and with great feeling" about the secession crisis. Kirkwood said that he "listened . . . with profound satisfaction" to Lincoln; however, he did not reveal the substance of the interview.[7]

Later in January, the Iowa legislature chose delegates to represent the state in the Washington Peace Conference the following month. Virginia had called the conference to recommend compromise provisions for congressional action on the secession crisis. In his instructions to the delegates, Kirkwood told them to avoid any compromise that would concede "all that the north has contended for and won" in the 1860 election. Such a compromise "would not bring peace," the governor declared. "The true policy for every citizen to pursue" in the crisis "is to set his face like flint against secession, to call it by its true name, treason." He correctly predicted that no good results would come from the Peace Conference or from a similar compromise introduced by Kentucky senator John J. Crittenden in Congress.[8] At the same time, Lincoln wrote to Illinois congressman William Kellogg that the instant the Republicans agreed to a compromise permitting the expansion of slavery, Sen. Stephen A. Douglas and proslavery men "have us under again, all our labor lost, and sooner or later must be done over." The president-elect impressed upon Sen. Lyman Trumbull, also of Illinois, the need to "stand firm. The tug has to come, & better now, than any time hereafter."[9]

Most of the Republican governors agreed that no compromise should be approved by Congress that yielded to Southern demands on slavery in the territories or acquiesced in secession. However, conservative Republican governors Morgan of New York and Curtin of Pennsylvania, sensitive to their states' commercial interests, hoped that Congress could reach an agreement containing constitutional amendments acceptable to both North and South. "If the loyal States are just and moderate, without any sacrifice of right or self-respect," Curtin argued, "the threatened danger may be averted." Faced with the nearby presence of slave states, the Keystone State governor in his inaugural speech of January 15 declared that the Republicans "had no design to interfere with or abridge the rights of the people of other States," a conciliatory position that Lincoln also took in his inaugural address on March 4. Curtin reminded Pennsylvanians, "There is nothing in the life of Mr. Lincoln, nor in any of his acts or declarations before or since his election, to warrant the apprehension that his administration will be unfriendly to the local institutions of any of the States." The governor reinforced the Republican view that "ours is a national government. It has within its sphere of action all the attributes of sovereignty, and among these are the right and duty of self-preservation. . . . No part of the people, no State nor combination of States, can voluntarily secede from the Union, nor absolve themselves from their obligations to it. To permit a State to withdraw at pleasure from the Union . . . is to confess that our government is a failure."[10] Remarkably, this statement anticipated that of Lincoln's in his inaugural address.

Curtin maintained that "all of the requirements of the constitution must be obeyed." The federal government, he said, "must have power adequate to the enforcement of the supreme law of the land in every State." The governor announced, "It is the first duty of the national authorities to stay the progress of anarchy and enforce the laws." He promised that "at every hazard," Pennsylvania would give the federal authorities "an honest, faithful, and active support" in preserving the Union of the founders.[11]

Governor Charles S. Olden of New Jersey joined the four border slave state governors in insisting that a sectional compromise was the only way to restore the Union without an internecine civil war. New Jersey was the last Northern state to end slavery, having done so in 1804, and in 1860 it split its electoral votes between Douglas and Lincoln. Nonetheless, Olden emphatically proclaimed his support for the Union and contended that the people of his state were prepared to defend the Constitution and the laws under it.[12] The governors of the border slave states went farther: they sought, though unsuccessfully, to serve as peacemakers in the crisis and check the secessionist movement before it engulfed their states. Even Governor Claiborne F. Jackson, the ardent Southern rights' governor of Missouri, at first favored a middle policy between the North and the South, but only so long as Lincoln and the Republicans did not violate his state's sovereignty, a likely event in Jackson's view.[13] The border state governors wanted a compromise that would reaffirm, in the form of a constitutional amendment, the protection of slavery in the South. They also wanted the upper North states to repeal their personal liberty laws designed to prevent the return of fugitive slaves to their masters. Except for Jackson, the border state governors did not threaten secession if the compromise movement failed.

The New England governors, as expected, had no faith in a compromise over the sectional troubles, which, they probably correctly believed, would be one-sided and in favor of the slave states. Still, all of the free states except Michigan, Minnesota, Wisconsin, California, and Oregon sent delegates to the Peace Conference in Washington in February. The seceded states of the lower South ignored the call for the conference. Andrew of Massachusetts, New England's most influential governor, reluctantly and in spite of the opposition of Charles Sumner, the state's radical U.S. senator, appointed delegates to the conference. As Governor Buckingham of Connecticut explained, his state's participation in the conference would demonstrate to Virginia and the border states that Connecticut was acting in good faith toward the South. The New England representatives, as well as most Northern delegates who had been appointed by Republican governors, voted against the proslavery compromise measures recommended by the Peace Conference.[14]

Buckingham probably reflected the position of the upper North governors when he wrote the president-elect one month before the Peace Conference. "I shall give your administration my earnest and cordial support," he told Lincoln. "I also trust you will be able to execute the laws all over our land in spite of the combinations of traitors" who were determined to resist the government. The Connecticut governor urged the president-elect to approach slavery as a "wholly national" issue, and not merely an issue for the states to determine. Like other upper North governors, Buckingham refused to recommend that his legislature repeal his state's personal liberty laws protecting fugitive slaves.[15]

The free state governors of the old Northwest (today's Midwest), particularly those whose states bordered on slavery, feared that the secession fever would spread to their states if left unchecked. They insisted that the incoming president adopt a hardline policy against Southerners who sought to destroy the Union. Declaring that the secessionists were traitors, western governors like William Dennison of Ohio and Oliver P. Morton of Indiana demanded that all federal laws should be enforced in the South. Dennison from the beginning of the crisis proved extremely sensitive to the economic impact that the rebel blockage of the transportation arteries to the Gulf of Mexico would have on his state. In early 1861, he adamantly declared that Ohio would not permit the secessionists to cut off the Ohio and Mississippi Rivers from its commerce. At the same time, he sought the approval of his legislature for the expansion of the state militia. Still, like other lower North governors, Dennison, as a concession to the South, appealed to the upper North states to repeal their personal liberty laws, albeit unsuccessfully. The Ohio governor also urged Lincoln to reaffirm the rights of the

Southern states to maintain unimpaired their domestic institutions, meaning slavery.[16]

In neighboring Indiana, Governor Morton decried any compromise with treason and ominously predicted the inevitability of war. The governor was ahead of most Hoosiers in demanding that the new president use federal power against those "traitors" who persisted in violating the laws of the land. Believing that all of the slave states would eventually leave the Union, Morton moved to prepare Indiana for a military confrontation on the Ohio River where it bordered on Kentucky. He feared that the secessionists would invade his state once war began. The rebels, with support in southern Indiana, would then overwhelm the state's Unionists. After Lincoln became president, but before the fighting in Charleston Harbor in April, Morton went to Washington and promised the new president six thousand troops for the suppression of the Southern insurrection. The governor became upset when Lincoln, wanting to avoid a conflict with the seceded states, refused to accept the troops.[17]

Lincoln waited until his inauguration to reveal his policy toward the secessionists in South Carolina and elsewhere in the lower South. On February 11, the president-elect left Springfield on a circuitous train route to Washington. For logistical reasons, he did not go to New England. Governors Morton, Dennison, Morgan, and Curtin greeted him in their states and approvingly heard him address their legislatures. From Harrisburg, Lincoln slipped through Baltimore in the middle of the night to avoid an attempt on his life. In Washington, he received a visit from Maryland governor Thomas H. Hicks, who cautioned him against the use of military force against the seceding states. Any hostile action against the South or slavery, Hicks warned Lincoln, would cause Virginia to leave the Union and would swing public opinion dangerously close to secession in Maryland and the other border states.[18]

By the time Lincoln took the oath of office on March 4, 1861, the central issue was no longer compromise, but rather federal coercion of the seven Southern states that had left the Union. The Republican governors insisted that Lincoln preserve national sovereignty in the

South. They wishfully hoped, however, that it could be done without military intervention and a war by a show of determination on the president's part to sustain the laws and maintain federal properties in the South.

In his long-awaited inaugural address, Lincoln outlined a policy toward the secessionists that waved both the olive branch and the threat of federal action to maintain the Union. Proclaiming that "the central idea of secession is the essence of anarchy," he announced that he could not recognize the seceded governments. He explained that if secession were "lawfully possible," it would destroy the stated purpose of the venerated founders "*to form a more perfect union.*" Lincoln declared that "no State, upon its own mere motion, can lawfully get out of the Union" and that "acts of violence, within any State or States, against the authority of the United States, are insurrectionary or revolutionary." "The power confided to me," he said, "will be used to hold, occupy, and possess the property, and places belonging to the government, and to collect the duties and imposts; but beyond what may be necessary for these objects, there will be no invasion—no using of force against, or among the people anywhere."[19]

The new president attempted to calm Southern fears, particularly about slavery. He reminded his "disaffected fellow countrymen," referring to the Southerners, of the "ample evidence" contained in his public speeches and his party platform that their property, peace, and personal security would be safe in his hands. "I have no purpose, directly or indirectly, to interfere with the institution of slavery in the States where it exists," he pledged. "I believe I have no lawful right to do so, and I have no inclination to do so." He also denounced John Brown–type raids into the South to free slaves, "no matter under what pretext, as among the gravest of crimes." Lincoln assured Southerners that he and his party were bound to enforce the Fugitive Slave Law, a position that the lower North and border state governors also supported. However, he refused to demand that the upper North states repeal their personal liberty laws protecting fugitives from slavery.[20]

Abraham Lincoln closed his inaugural address by appealing to the spirit of American patriotism among "disaffected" Southerners. "We must not be enemies," he told them. "Though passion may have strained, it must not break our bonds of affection. The mystic chords of memory, streching [*sic*] from every battle-field, and patriot grave, to every living heart and hearth-stone, all over this broad land, will yet swell the chorus of the Union, when again touched, as surely they will be, by the better angels of our nature."[21] These were stirring words that have become classic in Lincoln lore and Civil War literature. They also provided hope to many Americans in 1861 that under the new president's leadership, the crisis would be resolved and war averted.

Governor Morgan of New York probably reflected the view of most of his fellow Republican governors when he wrote to the new president on March 5: "I cannot let one day pass without expressing to you the satisfaction I have felt in reading and in considering the inaugural address. None can say, truthfully, they do not understand its meaning. Kind in spirit, firm in purpose, national in the highest degree, the points are all well made." Morgan assured Lincoln that "it cannot fail to command the confidence of the North, and the respect of the South."[22] On the other hand, Edward Everett, the distinguished orator and former governor of Massachusetts, wrote in his diary that, though the new president's tone in his address was "as conciliatory as possible," his intention to hold the forts and collect the duties in the seceded states would nevertheless "result in Civil War, which I am impelled to look upon as almost certain."[23] Everett's prediction proved tragically correct.

THE CALL TO ARMS

Lincoln's agonizing decision to sustain Fort Sumter in Charleston Harbor, followed by the Confederate bombardment of the fort, resulted in the formal surrender of the federal garrison on April 14. The next day, Lincoln issued a proclamation calling on the states for seventy-five thousand militiamen to suppress "combinations" in South Carolina and the lower South that were "too powerful to be suppressed by the ordinary course of judicial proceedings." The War Department established troop quotas for each state based on its population. North Carolina, Tennessee, Arkansas, and Virginia immediately took steps to leave the Union. The border slave states were traumatized by events and unsure of their future under the Republican regime. Unwilling at this time to provide men for the suppression of the Southern insurrection, the border states rejected the president's call for troops but remained in the Union. After Lincoln promised that Delaware and Maryland troops would be asked only to defend their states and the District of Columbia, Governors William Burton and Thomas H. Hicks agreed to tender their states' quota of militiamen to the War Department. By the end of 1861, Maryland as well as the other border states was providing troops for the Union army, while a minority of Maryland men donned the Confederate gray.[1]

The free states' response to Lincoln's April 15 proclamation appealing for troops proved entirely different from that of the border states. With only a slight exaggeration, all of the Northern governors reported to the president and Secretary of War Simon Cameron that their people were united in support of Lincoln's policy to suppress the Southern rebellion and meet his call for troops. "Great rejoicing here over your proclamation," Ohio governor William Dennison excitedly informed Lincoln. He promised that Ohio would furnish the largest number of men of any state. Governor Richard Yates of Lincoln's home state dispatched William Butler, an old friend of the president's, to Washington with a letter announcing, "Our people burn with patriotism and all parties show the same alacrity to stand by the Government and the laws of the country." They "are anxiously waiting" instructions and arms for the troops, Yates wrote. Even the Democrats, several governors reported, had joined in supporting the proclamation and raising troops for the Union cause.[2]

Lincoln's call for troops had not been made when Minnesota governor Alexander Ramsey on April 14 tendered one thousand men to the "General Government" to avenge the attack on Fort Sumter. Iowa governor Samuel J. Kirkwood, who had received the news of Lincoln's proclamation while caring for his livestock, told Simon Cameron on April 16, "Nine-tenths of the people here are with you, and will be so long as a similar [and firm] policy is followed." He indicated that fifteen to twenty volunteer companies had been immediately raised for the army. The Iowa governor even moved his office to Davenport, at the end of the telegraph line, where he would have immediate contact with Lincoln and the War Department. Like most Northern governors, Kirkwood spoke at mass rallies supporting the war and encouraging volunteering in the state units.[3]

Led by the Northern governors, spirited war preparations swept the states during the spring and summer of 1861. The Far West governors of California and Oregon, however, did not receive the April call for troops. Like Governor Beriah Magoffin in Kentucky, who refused Lincoln's requisition for men, Democratic governor John Whiteaker of Oregon proclaimed his state's neutrality in the war. In New York, Republican governor Edwin Morgan, even before he had received the details regarding Lincoln's call for troops, secured his legislature's approval for the enrollment of thirty thousand two-year volunteers and the strengthening of the state's military board.

New Jersey governor Charles Olden, though politically opposed to Lincoln, acted quickly to meet his quota. The president made a point of praising Olden and his New Jersey militiamen for their "patriotic effort" to sustain the government.[4]

The New England governors also moved immediately to fulfill Lincoln's April 15 call for troops. On the same day, Governor Andrew of Massachusetts telegraphed the War Department, "Dispatch received. By what route shall I send?" Irvin McDowell, assistant adjutant general of the U.S. Army in Washington, promptly replied, "Send your companies here by railroad."[5] Andrew raised three thousand militiamen, placed them under the command of Brigadier General Benjamin F. Butler, and dispatched them to defend the national capital from an expected rebel assault. Andrew supplied Butler's men from state military stores for the mission to save the city and the Lincoln government. While marching through Baltimore on April 19, seven companies of the Massachusetts troops were attacked by an infuriated crowd. This "skirmish" left four soldiers dead, three dozen injured, and caused numerous civilian casualties before the regiment moved on to Washington. Butler and the remainder of the Massachusetts units landed unopposed at Annapolis, despite the strong protest of Governor Hicks. On April 25, Butler's troops took the train to the national capital, where, much to the relief of Lincoln, they lifted the secessionist "siege" of the city.[6]

That morning, Andrew wrote to Secretary of War Cameron that he could send four thousand more troops if requisitioned. The difficulty of accepting the troops at this time, Cameron pointed out, was supplying and arming them. During the electrifying days after Fort Sumter and before the Lincoln administration could act, the Massachusetts governor became the virtual war minister of New England. Andrew and his fellow governors obtained loans from state banks and citizens to provide rations, tents, and other supplies for the troops. U.S. Army general John E. Wool, commanding the Department of the Northeast, gave the energetic Andrew the authority to garrison the forts in Boston Harbor and arm three vessels for the protection of the coast.[7]

Within ten days of the president's April 15 call for troops, several governors informed Lincoln and the War Department that they had exceeded their states' militia quotas. The outpouring of men proved especially impressive in the populous lower North states of Ohio, Indiana, Illinois, and Pennsylvania, which all bordered on the slave states and where fears of disloyalty were rampant. On April 23, Governor Morton of Indiana reported to the War Department that he had raised more than his state's quota to meet the emergency and had already dispatched troops to the Ohio River border with Kentucky. There, he revealed, "the people are much alarmed, [and are] forming companies, and demanding arms, which we have none to give."[8] A similar response came from Governor Yates of Illinois, who worried about the safety of the strategic river port of Cairo and other "Little Egypt" or Southern communities. On April 25, Yates wrote to Secretary of War Cameron that he "was greatly embarrassed by the number of volunteers which have assembled" in the state, far exceeding Illinois's quota. Many of the men, the Illinois governor said, had been dispatched to Cairo, where there was no qualified officer to muster them into the service and no arms to fight the insurgents. However, Yates insisted, "to send these men home will have a demoralizing effect." He also wanted the government to take additional Illinois regiments.[9]

Likewise, Governor Dennison of Ohio saw an immediate need for troops on his state's border. He strongly urged the president and the War Department to accept more troops from his state than Lincoln had called for. Dennison reported "a common expectation" in the southern Ohio counties that the area would become "a base for important operations" by secessionists. Hearing nothing from Lincoln or the War Department about his request, the Ohio governor reported to Secretary Cameron, and thus to Lincoln, that he had assumed "extraordinary responsibilities" in raising and organizing state troops. Dennison claimed that the "ardor of the people" would be "seriously repressed" if the War Department did not accept more troops than the president had requisitioned. Meanwhile, Governor Charles Robinson of the new state of Kansas frantically called on the Lincoln administration for arms to defend his state from an expected resurgence of attacks by Missouri "border ruffians."[10]

Taking advantage of the outpouring of support for the war, and now realizing that suppression of the rebellion would be no easy task, Lincoln on May 3 called for 42,034 three-year volunteers to be raised by the states. These troops were in addition to the 75,000 militiamen in his April 15 requisition. The president also authorized an expansion of the regular army by 22,714 men and the navy by 18,000. (There were only about 16,000 regular troops at this time; many were on the frontier and under officers who were resigning to join the Confederate army. Enlisted men could not resign from the old army.) When Congress met on July 4 at his summons, Lincoln informed it of his action and remarked, "These measures, whether strictly legal or not, were ventured upon, under what appeared to be a popular demand, and public necessity; trusting, then as now, that Congress would readily ratify them," which it did. Lincoln further announced, "It is believed that nothing has been done beyond the constitutional competency of Congress."[11]

Again, the governors, with the exception of those of the border states, responded with alacrity in the enrollment of the three-year volunteer regiments. However, they immediately faced massive problems of organizing, equipping, arming, and establishing camps for the units, in addition to those for the militiamen under the April 15 requisition. Governor Morgan of New York expressed a common concern when he wrote to Secretary of War Cameron, "I believe that the entire force" of the state "will be mustered into service sooner than they can be uniformed and equipped."[12] Morgan and the other governors thought that, as they were closer to the ground in the mobilization of the army than the small War Department in faraway Washington, they were in a better position to deal with the complexities of raising the regiments. However, the governors and Cameron found themselves overwhelmed by the tasks at hand. During the first months of the war, the War Department did not have the wherewithal to handle the organization, nor did it have the experience needed to create a substantial military force and place it in the field. Lincoln and officials in the War Department had to begin virtually from scratch in organizing a large army, including a unified command, that would be capable of penetrating the South and putting down the rebellion. They depended on state and local officials, especially the governors, to raise the forces necessary to conduct the war. The governors, except for those in border states during the first months of the war, would not be found wanting.

President Lincoln lacked experience in administration, and neither was he knowledgeable in overseeing the mobilization of a military force. His strength was as a political leader, which ultimately proved invaluable in gaining and retaining the cooperation of governors who were sensitive to their traditional prerogatives and to the constitutional authority of the states. In 1861, Secretary of War Cameron had the primary responsibility for coordinating the war effort with the states. It soon became clear that he was incapable of handling the arduous tasks associated with the organization and deployment of a national army, though he seemed to have been conscientious in his efforts. In his defense, for several months Cameron had available only limited resources. At the beginning of the war, he had about ninety people in the War Department to accomplish the unprecedented and thankless task of organizing the large army. Winfield Scott, the general in chief of the U.S. Army, was old and lacked the energy to handle the challenging mobilization problems that developed with the governors and other state officials.

In 1861, the governors bombarded Lincoln and Cameron with demands for arms, provisions, and transportation for the state troops that they had hurriedly raised and placed in substandard camps. Iowa governor Kirkwood wrote to General John E. Wool, who controlled the U.S. arsenal in Springfield, Massachusetts, that his state was almost "destitute of arms," and what it had received in the annual distribution of weapons from the federal arsenals was "so small and so utterly disproportioned to our actual population." These arms, Kirkwood lamented, were useless flintlock muskets. The weapons recently sent to Iowa from the Springfield arsenal, he charged, had been seized by Governor Yates for his troops when they entered Illinois. Furthermore, Kirkwood claimed, Yates had taken more than his state's share of arms from the Saint Louis arsenal, and the Illinois governor had inconsiderately refused to give Iowa any of them.[13]

Kirkwood, along with the governors of Minnesota, Wisconsin, and Kansas, had another problem—defending the state's frontier against "large bodies of Indians." In the same letter to General Wool, the Iowa governor reported to the War Department that the Indians in the northwestern part of the state had become "excited by the news that our country is engaged in civil war" and were preparing to take advantage of the situation. Kirkwood wrote that he was "daily in receipt of letters" indicating that "the danger of an attack by the Indians [was] imminent."[14] Kirkwood also contended that his state faced a threat from secessionists on the Missouri border who planned to challenge Unionists in southern Iowa. Although the danger was exaggerated, clashes with both Indians and rebels did occur in Iowa during the Civil War. Despite the demands of local defense, the state never had to draft men under the militia conscription legislation of 1862 or the federal conscription act of 1863; Iowa was able to meet its quota of troops with volunteers.

In Minnesota, fears of an Indian uprising did eventually become a harsh reality in 1862. Farther south, in 1861 the evacuation of federal forts in the Indian Territory (Oklahoma) and the western part of Kansas left the Union's newest state exposed to raids by both pro-Confederate forces and Great Plains Indians. Kansas governor Charles Robinson, a Republican, also faced brutal invasions from proslavery Missouri marauders. To counter these threats, Robinson received an authorization from the War Department to fill his state's quota with three regiments and use them for home defense.[15]

Meanwhile, that spring, the Northern governors called their legislatures into special sessions to obtain appropriations for the troops. Most of the legislatures quickly approved the funds to purchase arms and equipment for their state forces, though not in Ohio until after a "violent debate" over a large request for $1 million by Governor Dennison. Morton of Indiana immediately sent an agent to the Northeast and to Canada for the purchase of weapons and accoutrements, using what credit the state could provide. Governor Kirkwood actually extended his personal credit to help clothe three Iowa regiments, only to be bluntly notified by his bankers when the notes fell due. In other states, bankers and merchants, at the requests of the governors, proved generous in providing loans and gifts for the purchase of war goods. Governors, along with the agents of the War Department, found themselves competing with each other for the available arms on the market. This competition inevitably led to soaring prices and large profits for those involved in the weapons and equipment trade.[16]

By May, the governors had become impatient with the Lincoln administration's war preparations and policies. The lower North governors, whose states bordered on the slave states, became increasingly anxious about the inadequate defenses of their communities from rebel assaults. In addition, the protection of commerce from an anticipated blockage by the secessionists created equal or even greater concern for the governors in the West. Already, with the secession of the lower South, the governors in the Mississippi-Ohio River basin foresaw the curtailment of trade, much of which went through New Orleans and, to a lesser extent, Mobile. Despite the rapid prewar development of railroad and canal connections with the East, the western states still depended on the "Father of Waters" along with its ports and hinterland for their prosperity. (Later in the war, the demand for foodstuffs and other goods for the Union armies reduced these states' dependence on the Southern markets and outlets to the sea.)

The governors of Ohio, Indiana, and Illinois feared that Kentucky, led by Governor Beriah Magoffin, a strong Southern rights' supporter, would fall to the secessionists. Soon after the war began, the Bluegrass State adopted a policy of armed neutrality, which its neighboring free-state governors concluded would be a threat to the Union and their communities. The governors believed that unless the Lincoln government made a greater effort to prosecute the war in the West, their section would be forced to look outside of the old Union for their military and economic needs. The concept of a northwestern confederacy had already occurred to many people in the region, especially Democrats, who hated the thought of remaining under a government dominated by antislavery men and northeastern capitalists. As a product of the West, Lincoln understood the important interests of the region, but during the early part of the war, he had only limited means to address western concerns. He also had critical problems in the East to contend with.

Concerned about the stagnation in war preparations, Governor Dennison of Ohio invited the governors west of New England to meet in Cleveland on May 4, 1861. Dennison's purpose for the meeting was to pressure Lincoln and the War Department to take more vigorous measures to suppress the rebellion and protect their region. No border slave state governor was invited to the conference. Several governors immediately responded to the invitation, and they either attended the Cleveland conference or sent a representative.[17]

Of the eastern governors, only Curtin of Pennsylvania made the trip to Cleveland. Morgan of New York sent a close friend, John Bigelow, to represent his state. Yates of Illinois, pleading that he was too busy raising troops and attending to other state business, dispatched former lieutenant governor Gustave Koerner to represent the state at Cleveland. Koerner, Illinois's leading German American, arrived too late to participate in the conference. However, he later met with Governors Dennison and Morton and expressed Illinois's grave concerns about the slowness of federal preparations for the war, despite the enthusiasm in Illinois and other western states for volunteering to fight. Governors Austin Blair of Michigan and Alexander W. Randall of Wisconsin also participated in the conference. Two other western governors, Kirkwood of Iowa and Alexander Ramsey of Minnesota, did not attend the conference, probably because of the short notice and the long distance involved in traveling to Cleveland. Likewise, the governors of California, Oregon, and Kansas remained at home. George B. McClellan, whom Dennison had appointed to command Ohio troops, attended the conference. As was his intention, the ambitious McClellan made a good impression on the governors, who sought his military advice in the crisis.[18]

Dennison began the Cleveland conference by describing the dire situation that, he said, the Union and his state faced. He charged that Governor Magoffin of Kentucky, though professing neutrality while remaining in the Union, was "a traitor and was arming his State as fast as he could to resist the Union." According to Bigelow, who provided a firsthand account of the meeting, Dennison "produced satisfactory evidence" that Magoffin had obtained $200,000 worth of guns from the rebel governor of Louisiana for the purpose of over-powering the Unionists in his state and carrying the war across the Ohio River.[19] Actually, Magoffin, though a strong Southern rights' advocate, was walking a tightrope while maintaining Kentucky's policy of armed neutrality and staying in the Union. He remained tenuously loyal until August 1862, when, under pressure from ardent Unionists, he resigned as governor.

The Ohio governor complained to his Northern colleagues at Cleveland that the War Department had provided no information on its plans to protect the state's border with Kentucky and western Virginia. Exasperated by the Lincoln administration's inaction, Dennison, who later served as Lincoln's postmaster general, announced his intention to send two representatives to Washington "to present the facts to the Government and ascertain whether it meant to prosecute the war aggressively or simply . . . to do as little as possible to hurt the feelings of the South." Dennison informed the governors that he had twenty thousand soldiers ready to fight for their government, but "they would not be content to spend all summer lazing in camp, nor would he ask them to." He was unwilling "to answer for the loyalty of the Northwest if this policy of neglect was continued much longer." "We must defend ourselves if we are not defended" by the national government, he declared. Dennison specifically wanted the Lincoln administration to give him permission to march into Kentucky and western Virginia with Ohio troops and put down the secessionists. He also wanted a western division of the federal army organized with McClellan in command. Finally, he demanded that the federal government enforce a no-trade policy with the rebel states.[20]

The participants in the Cleveland conference agreed wholeheart-edly with Dennison. At the conclusion of the meeting, they asked Governor Alexander W. Randall of Wisconsin to write to President Lincoln expressing their concerns and views on the conduct of the war. They also agreed to send representatives or "messengers" to

Washington to plead the case for a greater military effort. Randall, who soon would be elected by his state's legislature to the U.S. Senate, wrote a long report to the president on May 6. The "messengers" were dispatched by the governors "to confer with you" on all issues relating to the West, he informed Lincoln. "The extreme anxiety we feel, and the anxiety felt by the people of the [free] border and Northwestern States, must be our sufficient warrant for urging some more definite course of policy in regard to the relations between the Government and these States." The governors, Randall assured Lincoln, "are pre-pared . . . to sustain you and your Administration in every measure, however extreme, for the suppression of this untoward rebellion and for the punishment of the treason."[21]

Despite their criticism, Randall told the president, the governors "appreciate most fully the difficulties under which you [have] labored in taking the reins of Government at a time" when the Union was unprepared for war. "But now we wish to urge [upon] you the absolute necessity, since Washington is safe, of giving more attention to the country immediately contiguous to the line between the free and the slave States." Here "the fierceness of this wicked rebellion is to exhibit itself . . . more than anywhere." North of the line from Pittsburgh to the junction of the Ohio with the Mississippi River, Randall reported, "the country is almost entirely defenseless against an armed enemy." He raised the specter of Cincinnati and other river towns "utterly destroyed and the country about them laid waste, without the means of resistance." Furthermore, "it is a matter of absolute necessity, not only for the Northern border States but for all the Northwestern States, to be able to control the business and commerce of the Ohio River and the Upper Mississippi in order to reach a vital part of this rebellion." The fall of Cairo in southern Illinois, Randall reminded Lincoln, not only would be a strategic disaster for the Union, but also would deliver a serious blow to the legitimate trade of the Mississippi River and its tributaries.[22]

The governors asked Lincoln "to call into the field at once 300,000 men" with arms and ammunition to defend their states and sustain the laws in the South. Moreover, Randall wrote, the governors wanted "a better military organization and a military head" to coordinate the war effort, perhaps having McClellan in mind. "There is no occasion for the Government to delay, because the States themselves are willing to act vigorously and efficiently," he continued. "A spirit [had been] evoked by this rebellion among the liberty-loving people of the country that is driving them to action," and, Randall warned, if the federal government did not act, "they will act for themselves." Indeed, the Wisconsin governor ominously predicted, "If the Government does not at once shoulder this difficulty and direct [the] current, there will come something more than a war to put down rebellion—it will be a war between border States," free versus slave, "which will lose sight, for the time, of the Government."[23]

Lincoln must have been stunned by Randall's report on the Cleveland conference expressing the critical concerns of the western governors in particular and demanding action, although he believed that the governors' fears of Kentucky falling to the secessionists were exaggerated. Still, he realized that the political situation in Kentucky as well as Missouri could change dramatically if he acted precipitously and authorized a federal or Northern state intervention, as Governors Dennison and Morton wanted. Such a military action, Lincoln concluded, could propel Kentucky and possibly Missouri into the Southern Confederacy. However, he agreed with the governors that armed neutrality as proclaimed by Kentucky was "treason in effect."[24]

When Lincoln did not move quickly to control the Ohio River and, in their minds, secure Kentucky's loyalty, Dennison, Morton, and Yates hurriedly met in Indianapolis on May 24 to discuss the situation further and urge the adoption of a strategic plan for military action in the West. Unlike Lincoln's temperament, patience was not a virtue of the governors', though their worries about the war in the West were realistic. At the conclusion of the meeting, the governors prepared a "memorial" to General in Chief Winfield Scott expressing their views. They insisted that General McClellan, recently appointed as commander in the region, should be directed to secure the loyalty of Kentucky and then move against the rebel states. The three governors asked Scott to order Colonel Robert J. Anderson, late of Fort Sumter fame and soon to be a brigadier general, who was in command at Cincinnati, to raise and arm regiments of loyal men in his home state of Kentucky. They specifically wanted these troops to seize key points in Kentucky, including Louisville, immediately and gain control of the railroads leading south. They argued that the occupation of strategic positions in the Bluegrass State, and also in Tennessee and Missouri, could serve as bases for coordinated operations against the "more Southern States." "This course" of action, the governors insisted, "will save Kentucky to the Union; otherwise . . . the secessionists will control her."[25]

The western governors dispatched Yates to Washington to deliver the "memorial" to General Scott and urge immediate action. Although he had no military experience, Yates also wanted Lincoln to appoint him a major general in command of Illinois troops in the Union army. When a friend recommended the Yates appointment to Lincoln, the president wisely ignored the suggestion. Lincoln's failure to appoint him as a major general contributed to Yates's growing belief that his old political colleague was incapable of serving as president.[26]

Meanwhile, on May 29, General Scott, presumably after talking to the president, replied to the "memorial" from the three western governors. He agreed with them that a coordinated plan should be adopted against the rebellion in the lower Mississippi valley. During his visit to Washington, Yates had insisted that the river port of Memphis "ought to be immediately occupied" by western forces under General McClellan. General Scott told Yates and his colleagues that an expedition at this time against Memphis would be premature and "would sweep Ohio, Indiana, Illinois, &c." of volunteers, leaving those states without troops "for pushing the war to a close at the right season."[27]

General Scott, probably also after conferring with Lincoln, rejected the governors' demand that the War Department establish control of key points in Kentucky, Missouri, and Tennessee and intervene in the Bluegrass State to protect Unionists. Scott reminded the governors that to occupy Kentucky would violate the state's neutrality and achieve what they clearly did not seek—the secession of the state. He informed the governors that "the wisest and best Union men in Kentucky have strongly intimated that thrusting protection upon their people is likely to do far more harm than good."[28] One of these Union men was Lincoln's trusted friend Joshua Speed.

The western governors, however, continued to urge Lincoln and the War Department to send troops into Kentucky. No governor was more persistent than Morton in pressing for intervention. On September 2, 1861, he telegraphed the War Department, "At the risk of being considered troublesome, I will say the conspiracy to precipitate Kentucky into revolution is complete. The blow may be struck at any moment."[29] The Indiana governor became alarmed when he visited Louisville three weeks later and learned that rebel forces had entered Kentucky, seized the important Louisville and Nashville Railroad, and advanced within forty miles of Louisville. He excitedly telegraphed the president that if the troops were not driven immediately from the state, they would occupy Louisville, and Kentucky would be a rebel state "as completely as South Carolina." Morton also claimed that southern Indiana was defenseless because the federal government had failed to provide his state with sufficient arms. He even advised the president on what military tactics should be employed to dislodge the Confederates from Kentucky and save southern Indiana.[30]

Lincoln did not panic, but the Indiana governor's frenzied messages clearly concerned him. On September 29, the president wrote a long letter to Morton in which he attempted to reassure the governor that neither Kentucky nor Indiana was endangered by the rebel invasion. "It is true," the president explained, "the Army in our front may make a half circle around Southward, and move on Louisville; but when they do, we will make a half circle around Northward, and meet them, and in the mean time we will get up what forces we can from other sources to also meet them." On the issue of arms for Indiana, Lincoln informed the governor, "You do not receive arms from us as fast as you need them . . . because we have not near enough to meet all the pressing demands; and we are obliged to share around what we have, sending the larger share to the points which appear to need them most. We have great hope that our own supply will be ample before long, so that you and all others can have as many as you need."[31]

"As to Kentucky," Lincoln told Governor Morton, "you do not estimate that state as more important than I do; but I am compelled to watch all points. While I write this I am, if not in *range*, at least in *hearing* of cannon-shot, for an army of enemies more than a hundred thousand strong," an inflated number the federal commanders in Virginia apparently had given him. "I do not expect [the rebels] to capture this city," he continued; "but I *know* they would, if I were to send the men and arms from here, to defend Louisville." Morton found incredible Lincoln's statement that "there is not a single hostile armed soldier within forty miles, nor any force known, to be moving upon [Louisville] from any distance."[32] The president's letter did little to reassure Morton and the other Northern governors bordering on the Ohio River about the rebel threat, since a Confederate army under General Albert Sidney Johnston had occupied a large swath of southern Kentucky and would soon establish a pro-Confederate state government at Bowling Green.[33] Lincoln, however, was correct about Louisville. Despite recurring threats, the city never fell to Confederate forces during the war.

With Confederate armies gathering in northern Virginia and in the Mississippi valley during the summer, President Lincoln agreed with the western governors in Randall's report that the number of volunteers should be increased dramatically over those called soon after Fort Sumter. On July 4, 1861, Lincoln asked Congress for the authority to raise at least four hundred thousand men and for $400 million to support the war. Such an appropriation, he contended, would make "this contest a short, and a decisive one. A right result, at this time, will be worth more to the world, than ten times the men, and ten times the [requested] money."[34]

On July 22, the day after the Union disaster at the First Battle of Bull Run, a shocked but determined Congress approved what the president wanted—and more—providing for five hundred thousand three-year volunteers. Three days later in a supplementary bill, it authorized an additional five hundred thousand, followed by another increase in the regular army. Congress also enacted a series of revenue measures to support the military, including an income tax and borrowing through the sale of Treasury notes.[35] The two bills expanding the volunteer army reinforced the governors' primary role in the mobilization and organization of the forces. The July 22 act specifically provided that "the Governors of the States . . . shall commission the field, staff, and company officers" for the volunteers. Fred A. Shannon, in the standard account on the Union army's organization, wrote, "The principle of state rights, as applied to the raising of the army, had prevailed. The federal government might call for the troops and assign the quotas, but the states would raise the men, organize the regiments, and, to a great extent, control their destinies."[36]

Several governors soon protested to Lincoln that their states did not receive a fair share of brigadier generals. Kirkwood of Iowa became particularly incensed that troops from his state were serving under Illinois generals. On December 4, he wrote to Lincoln that it was demoralizing for Iowa troops and the people of the state, who had contributed more than their quota of soldiers, to be treated in such a fashion. He pointed out to the president that only two Iowans had been appointed as brigadier generals, and none as a major general. Lincoln, whose practice it was to ignore such letters lest his response further inflame the situation, did not reply to the governor. Kirkwood then complained to Iowa senator James W. Grimes, then in Washington, about the president's failure to answer his letter, vowing that he would persist in his efforts for fair treatment in appointments to military command.[37]

When Morton of Indiana learned that his state's congressional delegation had bypassed him and nominated men as brigadier generals, he protested to Lincoln. The governor indignantly informed the president that he "had much more to do with the officers than any members of Congress and . . . had much more responsibility in connection with the organization than any of them."[38] Morton continued, with limited success, to complain to Lincoln about the appointment of Indiana brigadier generals whom he judged incompetent or politically undesirable.[39]

Some governors who had organized a large number of state troops, such as Curtin of Pennsylvania, Yates of Illinois, and Dennison of Ohio, wanted a hand in the selection of major generals as department commanders.[40] The president, however, was careful to control appointments of senior generals. When Governor Yates and William

Butler, an old Lincoln friend, sought the promotion of John Pope of Illinois to the rank of major general in the regular army after his capture of Island No. 10 in the Mississippi River in April 1862, the president refused their suggestion, writing, "I fully appreciate Gen. Pope's splendid achievements . . . but you must know that Major Generalships in the Regular Army, are not as plenty as blackberries."[41] Actually, in the case of Island No. 10, a naval force consisting of six ironclads and ten mortar boats probably had more to do with this Union military success than Pope's generalship.

A more serious controversy over the army's mobilization erupted when Lincoln and the War Department disregarded the authority of the governors to raise and organize regiments under the July 1861 acts of Congress expanding the volunteer army. On August 21, Governor Curtin wrote a long, troubling letter to the president bringing the issue to his intention. He complained that "unfortunately the Government of the United States" was authorizing individuals to raise regiments in his state independent of the governor and in conflict with the legislation of Congress and with Pennsylvania law. "Fifty-eight individuals [had] received authority for this purpose in Pennsylvania," Curtin angrily told Lincoln. "The direct authority of the [federal] Government," he said, had been "set in competition with that of the State, acting under its requisition" for troops. "The consequence has been much embarrassment, delay, and confusion." Curtin reported that, although fragments of seventy state regiments had been filled, the result of the War Department's policy was "that after the lapse of twenty-six days not one entire regiment has been raised in Pennsylvania since the [July] requisition." Nonetheless, Curtin, a strong supporter of the war, promised to "leave the authorities of the United States to construe their own law" and assured Lincoln that, if he found it necessary, he would "take responsibility of disobeying" the Pennsylvania law. He would do this "rather than fail in any effort that may be required" to mobilize the state's military force "in such manner as the Government of the United States may point out."[42]

Meanwhile, reports had also reached Governor John A. Andrew of Massachusetts that the War Department had given permission "to individuals to raise regiments . . . independently of and conflicting with the regular recruiting system of the Commonwealth." He immediately wrote his two agents in Washington to demand that the War Department reverse the decision. On September 4, 1861, the agents met with Secretary Cameron, who, as they reported to Andrew, agreed with them that the authority to recruit independently of state authorities should be denied. Cameron expressed "his determination that none should be issued hereafter."[43]

The next day, Governor Andrew's representatives conferred with the president on the issue. They reported that Lincoln "stated his concurrence in [Cameron's] opinion that no more independent permissions to raise regiments should be granted to individuals" in the states. Lincoln admitted, according to Andrew's agents, that such "permissions as had hitherto been issued had been extorted by the pressure of certain persons, who, if they had been refused, would have accused the Government of rejecting the services of so many thousands of imaginary men—a pressure, of the persistency of which, no person not subjected to it could conceive." The president acknowledged that "perhaps he had been in error in granting" the authority, "even under this pressure."[44]

In ending the interview with Andrew's agents, the president noted that a few days earlier, Governor Morgan of New York had visited the White House and complained of the independent recruiting practices in his state. Lincoln, however, said that he had reached an "arrangement" with Morgan "to obviate all these difficulties" and added, it "might be necessary to apply the same remedy to the other States."[45] The "arrangement" with the Empire State governor was formalized by the War Department on the same day as the interview with Andrew's representatives. "All persons having received authority to raise" troops in New York, it directed, "will immediately report" to Governor Morgan the status of their units. "They and their commands" will be "placed under the orders" of the governor, "who will reorganize them and prepare them for service in the manner he may judge most advantageous for the interests of the General Government."[46] Curtin of Pennsylvania also seemed satisfied with the arrangement.[47]

On September 10, 1861, Lincoln granted General Benjamin F. Butler a similar arrangement, but for a broader area than one state.

He authorized Butler "to raise, organize, arm, uniform and equip a Volunteer force for the War, in the New England States," though not to exceed six regiments. Butler, who spent much of the Civil War involved in controversies of his own making, would command the force. Lincoln made it clear, however, that the permission to raise the regiments was "to be of no effect, unless the Governor of each State from which troops are to be enlisted, shall indorse his approval upon it."[48] Anxious to avoid any misunderstanding regarding the authority of the New England governors, the next day the president sent a message to them with the official notification of the Butler authorization and asking the governors to answer him by telegraph if they consented to it. All of the governors approve the arrangement with the general, including Andrew, who, moved by the patriotic enthusiasm of the moment, immediately agreed to "help General Butler to the utmost."[49] The Massachusetts governor soon regretted his endorsement of Butler's undertaking.

Butler had no intention of conceding control to the governors in raising and organizing the troops for his independent command. Although most of the New England governors acquiesced in Butler's undermining of their authority in the matter, Governor Andrew did not. Andrew had crossed political swords with Butler before the war. (Prewar state political rivalries often reasserted themselves during the Civil War.) The issue over recruitment became heated in October 1861, when the general announced the creation of the Department of New England and provocatively established his headquarters within sight of the governor's office in Boston. Butler began to enlist men for two regiments in Massachusetts, and he declared that they would receive state aid. Andrew refused to approve it because, he argued, only the governor had the authority to pay bona fide state troops, which Butler's men were not. The irascible general, who was a hero among Republicans in Washington for lifting the rebel siege of the city in the spring, countered by securing funds from the War Department to finance the troops.[50]

Butler then attempted to force Andrew's hand into sanctioning his regiments by asking the governor to sign the commissions of the officers he had chosen. Andrew refused, however, citing as his authority

Lincoln's order and also the July 22 Act of Congress. When that failed, Butler sent to the Massachusetts legislature for its approval a list of officers from a sea battery. He claimed that the battery had earlier been raised under the authority of the state. When Governor Andrew later received the list, he defiantly declined to commission the officers.[51]

At this point, the two powerful New Englanders had reached an impasse in the conflict, highlighted by a lengthy tit-for-tat correspondence between the men and their subordinates. The quarrel became petty. Andrew, for example, refused a request by the general for rooms in the State House for his offices. Not to be outdone, Butler had his adjutant general reject a letter sent to him by the governor's military secretary because it did not contain Andrew's signature.[52] The dispute between the governor and the general was particularly unseemly in view of the nation's effort in 1861 to organize its full military strength to fight the war. Inevitably, both sides appealed to authorities in Washington for support.

On November 18, General Butler complained to U.S. adjutant general Lorenzo Thomas that Andrew was the only New England governor who had refused to aid his recruitment efforts. He told Thomas that Andrew, in rejecting his authority to enroll troops in Massachusetts, had declared, "in substance, that the President of the United States had no right to recruit" men in his state. "This doctrine of secession did not seem to me any more sound uttered by a Governor north of Mason and Dixon's line than if proclaimed by Governor Magoffin, south, so that I paid no heed to it," Butler claimed. "The question of utmost moment" for the Lincoln administration was, would it allow the authority to recruit and organize federal forces "wrested from [it] by the States?"[53] The troublesome general also went to Washington to pressure Lincoln and Secretary of War Cameron to force Andrew to approve his regiments and commission their officers.

On his part, Governor Andrew directed his state agents in Washington to meet with Lincoln and Secretary of War Cameron for the purpose of countering General Butler's efforts and demanding the disbandment of the Department of New England. Lincoln, for sound political reasons, did not want to repudiate the popular general.

Following a visit by Butler to the White House, Henry Lee, the governor's military aide-de-camp, talked to Lincoln. The president clearly hoped to avoid involvement in the controversy. On other occasions, specifically regarding political conflicts among Union leaders in Missouri and Maryland, Lincoln referred to such disputes as little more than "pestilent factional quarrel[s]," which, if he intervened, could easily assume national significance and damage the unity he sought in the war.[54] Lee reported to Andrew that the president "expressed his regret at the want of concert between" the governor and the general. Lincoln, however, suggested to Lee that it "was owing to [Andrew's] personal dislike" of Butler that the controversy had occurred. Lee insisted that this was not the case, pointing out that Butler's actions in Massachusetts only confirmed his reputation "as a factious man." Lincoln said that Lee had presented him with the alternatives either "to crush Butler or to prevail upon [Andrew] to forgive him and commission his officers." Lee sadly concluded in his report that neither the president nor the War Department was prepared "to crush Butler."[55]

A few days later, Massachusetts attorney general Dwight Foster saw the president and again unsuccessfully argued the governor's position. During the course of the interview, Lincoln facetiously remarked that "Genl. Butler was cross-eyed and he supposed he didn't see things as other people did." Andrew, who had virtually no sense of humor, was infuriated when he learned of the president's levity in the matter and the War Department's insistence that he commission Butler's officers.[56] On December 27, the governor angrily wrote to Adjutant General Thomas, "Nothing whatever has occurred to change my determination not to commission officers over these irregular troops." He especially objected to Butler's selection of Jonas H. French, a Democrat, and other old political cronies as officers in his regiments. Andrew reminded Thomas that after he had repeatedly protested "General Butler's insubordinate action" in the affair, the War Department should have realized that his refusal to commission the officers was "inevitable" and could "have spared this State the confusion, division, and distress to which it has been subjected by these irregular enlistments."[57]

Andrew asked Massachusetts senators Charles Sumner and Henry Wilson to intervene with Lincoln on his behalf and against Butler, though he was aware that the president did not want to repudiate the popular general. The governor also sent the extensive correspondence documenting the controversy for review by the president and other officials in Washington. Andrew denied to the senators, and thus to Lincoln, that he was acting out of personal spite toward Butler. He also maintained that it was not in his "temper to see the public service injured, our people distracted, and our military efficiency demoralized by proceedings at once unjust and discourteous" to the state. "But when the venerable Commonwealth," the governor wrote, "is thus treated with contumely," he could not "remain silent." "The whole course of proceedings" under Butler, Andrew unfairly charged, "have been designed [by] persons of bad character to make money unscrupulously, and to encourage men whose unfitness had excluded them from any appointment by me to the volunteer military service."[58]

After the Massachusetts senators circulated the documents in Washington, the tide turned in favor of Governor Andrew in the controversy with General Butler.[59] Contributing to the change was the resignation on January 11, 1862, of Cameron as secretary of war. Cameron had tacitly supported Butler in the dispute. On the same day, Lincoln telegraphed the governor, "I will be greatly obliged if you will arrange somehow with General Butler to officer his two unofficered regiments." Andrew replied that he would like to approve Butler's companies and regiments and some of their officers. However, there were names on the general's list of officers, he wrote, "whom I could not in conscience appoint, and whom to commission would offend both my sense of honor and of duty." The Republican governor reminded the president, "I have been silent [in] public" on the issue, "trusting that the Federal Government would at last discontinue the toleration of this indignity practiced toward a Commonwealth which had done nothing to deserve it." The threat was clear: he would appeal to the people in his state for support on the issue if Lincoln did not correct the situation.[60]

A few days later, Edwin M. Stanton, who, unlike Cameron, favored Andrew, became secretary of war. Probably after talking to Lincoln,

Stanton notified Frank Howe, another Andrew agent in the national capital, that the controversy could be easily settled if the governor came to Washington. Andrew, however, found it impossible to leave Boston immediately, despite a warning by Howe that Butler was in the capital and still pursuing "his snaky, slimy course" with Lincoln and other members of his administration. Meanwhile, Howe and Mrs. Andrew, who also was visiting in Washington, attended a public reception at the White House and were greeted by Lincoln. Taking Mrs. Andrew by the hand, the president asked, "Well how does your Husband and Butler get on—has the Governor commissioned these men yet?" When Mrs. Andrew hesitated, Howe answered, "We are informed Sir that you have commissioned them." "No," said Lincoln, "but I am getting mad with the Governor and Butler both." When Andrew's wife told him that he did not look very angry, the president responded, "No, I don't ever get fighting mad, no how."[61]

Finally, Andrew broke away from Boston and went to Washington. He quickly reached a satisfactory agreement with Stanton. The secretary of war assigned two officers of the regular army to the disputed regiments; in turn, the governor commissioned both and approved the regiments' rosters. Much to Andrew's delight, Butler's Department of New England was disbanded. The governor's triumph over the general was complete, though Butler breezily announced that the department had fulfilled its purpose of recruiting a force of New Englanders for the war, and for military reasons, he said, it had been "abrogated by the Department of War." On February 21, Butler left with his troops for Ship Island in the Gulf of Mexico. Although Lincoln earlier had expressed a desire to see him, Andrew refused to visit the White House when he was in Washington, even to attend a ball given by Mrs. Lincoln to which the governor and his wife were invited. The Bay State governor privately denounced the president's hadling of the controversy with Butler. Not until after the president's assassination did Andrew change his opinion, formed in 1861, that Lincoln lacked the essential qualities to lead the nation during the war.[62]

THE WAR BECOMES LONG

During the fall and winter of 1861–62, the mobilization of the Union armies proceeded through the governors. The goals established by Lincoln in the summer, however, were not completely achieved. Volunteers raised by the governors and the states reached 640,000 in December 1862, while the regular army barely increased by 4,000 over its prewar strength.[1] Fervor for the fighting and the novelty of life in the army had significantly declined, causing resistance to long-term enlistments to increase. The need for men at home to harvest crops and provide for their families as winter approached further contributed to the difficulties in raising troops. Governors continued to complain to Lincoln and the War Department about the lack of arms, provisions, and federal financial support for their regiments.

Gubernatorial authority over the state troops in the field created confusion as the Union armies moved into the South. David Tod of Ohio reflected this uncertainty after he replaced William Dennison as governor in January 1862. He asked the War Department "whether he had control of his state troops in camp and in the field after they had been mustered into federal service" and also wanted to know whether the U.S. Treasury would repay the states for "*all* the money expended directly and indirectly in the raising equipping, sustaining and mustering of the troops."[2] Much to the dismay of Tod, no clear answers to his questions were forthcoming from the War Department.

The concept of a national army, independent of the states and the governors, did not become a reality until much later in the war.[3] Secretary of the Treasury Salmon P. Chase, a former Ohio governor and the leading Radical Republican in Washington, announced at this time that he would "rather have no regiments raised in Ohio than that they should not be known as Ohio regiments."[4] The governors and state officials, however, conceded tactical authority over their state troops to the War Department and the commanding generals as they became part of a larger federal army. Still, they reserved the right to retain a close relationship with their troops in the South and to urge Lincoln and the War Department to replace generals they disliked, usually with generals from their own states.

As the war became hard in 1862, the Northern governors became more energetic and resourceful in attending to their troops in the field. Several governors visited their men in camps near rebel lines; others sent their military adjutants. Lincoln provided tacit support for these visits, though he did not seem to encourage them. He probably believed that, in addition to providing needed medical supplies and other material and personal assistance, the governors' appearances at the front boosted morale and increased support for the war at home. No one was more active in attending to the needs—and the morale—of the troops than Governor Morton. He frequently corresponded with Indiana officers and soldiers and sent state officials into the camps to determine their needs and ensure that they were met. However, General Henry W. Halleck, commander of the Western Department, did not appreciate the governor's interference. Halleck became involved in an unnecessary dispute with Morton over the governor's attempt to provide supplies for Indiana troops in his theater.[5]

As a result of Morton's efforts, the Indiana Sanitary Commission, a private aid society inspired by the creation of the U.S. Sanitary Commission in June 1861 and supported by Lincoln, was formed in March 1862. The Indiana Sanitary Commission, which remained independent of the national association, was criticized by the U.S. commission for its "indiscreet zeal" in recognizing "state lines even in its administration of mercy on the battlefield." For his attention to their needs, Indiana troops affectionately referred to Morton as "the soldiers' governor." On several occasions, Morton went south and bivouacked with the Union army in Tennessee and Mississippi. A soldier in the Army of the Cumberland wrote home, "You ought to hear the shouts of the soldiers from all states whenever Governor Morton is mentioned."[6]

Immediately after the horrific Battle of Shiloh (Pittsburg Landing) in western Tennessee in April 1862, Governors Morton, Yates of Illinois, and Louis P. Harvey of Wisconsin chartered steamboats; gathered surgeons, nurses, and medical supplies; and hurried to the site. The three governors assisted in administering to the needs of the wounded and providing transportation for many to recuperate in state hospitals. Governor Austin Blair of Michigan also brought aid when he visited his troops at Pittsburg Landing in May. Morton alone arranged for sixty surgeons and more than three hundred nurses to meet the wounded soldiers when they returned home. The western governors offered encouragement to the men who remained at the front to battle the Confederate army.[7]

Unfortunately, Governor Harvey of Wisconsin died in the effort to aid his state troops after the Battle of Shiloh. On a rainy night, as he prepared to return home with wounded soldiers, Harvey slipped on the steamboat gangplank near Pittsburg Landing, fell into the Tennessee River, and disappeared. Several days later, his body was found sixty-five miles downriver. Harvey, who had been governor of Wisconsin for only three months, was replaced by Lieutenant Governor Edward Salomon, a young refugee from the failed German democratic revolution of the late 1840s. Salomon, who served until 1864, apparently was the only Jewish governor during the Civil War.[8]

Governor Morton also joined General William Tecumseh Sherman in the vanguard of the Union army's advance from Shiloh to Corinth, Mississippi. Sherman later wrote that the governor rode with him every day and "was a close observer of the practical details of camp life." Morton "was as impatient as the rest of us at our slow and methodical, if not timid, advance," Sherman said. "We were short of wagons to bring from Pittsburg Landing the necessary supplies, and he wanted to send to Indiana for one thousand wagons and teams. The idea of war operations being delayed by the want of means easily procurable was a thorn in his side." If Morton's advice regarding the immediate necessity for provisions had been heeded by the War Department, Sherman believed, "we would have taken Vicksburg that summer and turned eastward to do the work which had to be done two years afterwards." The general remembered, "We at the front always felt more confident because we knew that Oliver P. Morton was at his post in Indianapolis, multiplying his efforts in the days of reverses and cheering us on in success."[9] Despite Morton's repeated demands on the president, Lincoln also came to appreciate the governor's dedicated leadership during the war.

In the spring of 1862, General George B. McClellan, now general in chief of the Union armies, launched his long-awaited offensive in Virginia against the Confederate army. Realizing that the Confederate forces risked encirclement, General Robert E. Lee, then President Jefferson Davis's military adviser in Richmond, recommended to General Thomas Jonathan Jackson, commanding a small army in the Shenandoah Valley, that he strike the Union forces in the area before McClellan could fully concentrate his troops for the assault elsewhere. Stonewall Jackson needed little encouragement to act. On May 8, he began a brilliant campaign by sweeping aside a force under John C. Frémont near Staunton and moving northward down the valley.[10]

Expecting an invasion of Maryland and the national capital by Jackson, the War Department sent an urgent message to all the governors except for those in the distant West. "Intelligence from various quarters leaves no doubt that the enemy in great force are advancing on Washington. You will please organize and forward immediately all the volunteer and militia force in your State."[11] The emergency, while exaggerated, seemed so great that Lincoln waived the War Department policy of accepting only three-year or duration-of-the-war volunteers.

Having believed that McClellan's army would soon defeat the rebel forces and occupy Richmond, the news from Washington startled the governors. Although they expressed a desire to provide the necessary troops, the governors pleaded that, because of the suddenness of the call, they could recruit, organize, and provide equipment and transportation for only a limited number of men. They reported to the War Department that their state treasuries were bare, and furthermore, their legislatures had gone home without appropriating additional funds for the war. Their states, the governors insisted, needed federal money in order to comply with the administration's call for more troops, including bonuses to attract volunteers. Governors Alexander Ramsey of Minnesota and Nathaniel S. Berry of New Hampshire also said that because the call for troops came during a busy farming season, men who were not already in the federal army would be reluctant to volunteer. Still, like other governors, Berry informed Secretary of War Stanton, "New Hampshire will cheerfully respond" to the call "to the extent of her ability to aid the Government in putting down this wicked and causeless rebellion."[12]

Edwin D. Morgan of New York, though governor of the richest state in the Union, complained of the dire financial situation that he faced in responding to the War Department's urgent request for men. He wrote to Stanton, "It is essential that I fully understand in what manner the expenses attending this duty shall be met." The New York legislature, Morgan revealed, had made no appropriations for the purpose of raising troops. "It will be necessary, therefore, for me to look wholly to the General Government, and I now ask that that Government at once assume the payment of all necessary expenses, and that all needful authority be formally issued to me."[13] The federal assumption of the financial burden for raising the troops, along with national military conscription in 1863–64, ultimately worked to undermine the Union governors' authority in the recruitment and organization of the state regiments.

Stonewall Jackson's expected offensive into Maryland and the District of Columbia in the spring of 1862 did not occur. Instead, Jackson rapidly moved his force of seventeen thousand to join Lee in the horrendous battles around Richmond against the main Union army under McClellan. In seven days of fighting, the "Young Napoleon" failed to take the Confederate capital or bring the rebellion closer to an end. The spring campaign on the Virginia peninsula, which extended into the summer, resulted in tremendous casualties and a growing disillusionment in the North over the war to restore the Union, with many starting to believe that it was not worth the losses and suffering. The carnage at Shiloh and Corinth in the western theater fed this dismay. Union successes in early 1862 at the Battle of Pea Ridge, Arkansas; the Confederate surrender of Forts Henry and Donelson to U. S. Grant; the easy capture of Nashville; and the fall of New Orleans in May only temporarily boosted morale. These victories were followed by a stalemate in the western campaign to suppress the insurrection in the lower South.

The manpower needs of both the eastern and western armies soared in mid-1862. Predictably, as the long lists of casualties circulated in the North, the War Department increasingly experienced problems obtaining new recruits and filling old regiments hit hard by enemy fire, capture, desertion, and disease.[14] Union troops who had enthusiastically volunteered at the beginning of the war now refused to reenlist, despite monetary incentives. Meanwhile, the Confederates were resorting to conscription to meet their manpower shortages.

In Indiana, Governor Morton excitedly reported to Secretary of War Stanton that "a secret political organization" had emerged in his state, whose "leading objects [were] to embarrass all efforts to recruit men for the Military service of the United States, to embitter public sentiment" against the war, and to "foster newspapers of extremely doubtful loyalty." The organization, Morton claimed, was "in operation in every county of the State." These "traitors," or peace militants, he charged, were "doing incalculable injury to the Union cause, not, it is true, openly and in plain terms, but by insidious, malignant and vituperative attacks upon Union men, those engaged in the Military Service, and those who are endeavoring to raise additional troops for our armies." Morton demanded that the federal government "take immediate, vigorous, and effective steps to break up these unlawful and dangerous combinations."[15] However, the Lincoln administration in 1862 took no action, probably believing that Morton, as was his tendency, had exaggerated the strength and tactics of the peace advocates in the state. Still, the Indiana antiwar movement heralded the rise of the Copperheads, which became the dominant faction in the Democratic Party in the state and elsewhere in the lower North.

Meanwhile, Lincoln clearly recognized the desperate need for additional troops in the aftermath of McClellan's retreat from around Richmond. He admitted to Secretary of State William H. Seward on June 28, "I would publicly appeal to the country for this new force, were it not that I fear a general panic and stampede would follow," in view of McClellan's failure. But not to be deterred by the army's setbacks and the political costs resulting from the long casualty lists, Lincoln reaffirmed to Seward that he would "maintain this contest until successful, or till I die, or am conquered, or my term expires, or Congress or the country forsakes me." He believed that with one hundred thousand new volunteers, McClellan could still take Richmond and "substantially end the war." The president looked to the governors to take the initiative in the important and difficult task of raising the necessary troops "in the shortest possible time."[16]

With that in mind, Lincoln dispatched Seward to New York to meet with governors Curtin of Pennsylvania and Morgan of New York. The secretary of state took with him a report from the president describing the military situation and asking the governors to issue a call in their states for the troops. Seward, along with his alter ego, Thurlow Weed, and the Union (War) Committee of New York, met with Curtin and Morgan on June 29. Rather than the governors' requisitioning the troops, as Lincoln wanted, Curtin and Morgan suggested that Seward draft a memorial to the president from the governors, asking Lincoln to call for 150,000 men, including 50,000 recently requested by Secretary of War Stanton.[17]

On July 1, Lincoln approved the proposed memorial. Curtin and Morgan immediately secured the agreement of all of the Union governors except for five who could not be reached at the time. Three of these governors eventually gave their approval; the Oregon and California executives apparently were never contacted. The border slave states' governors and Francis H. Pierpont of the Restored (Union) Government of Virginia, mainly western Virginia, also telegraphed their consent to the call for the troops. The memorial was backdated to June 28 to give it the fiction of having originated with the governors and in hopes of preventing a panicked response to McClellan's failure in the Seven Days' campaign to capture the Confederate capital.[18]

Encouraged by the governors' strong support, on July 1 Lincoln issued a call for three hundred thousand volunteers rather than the two hundred thousand in the original plan.[19] Stanton immediately dispatched General Catharinus P. Buckingham to confer with the governors in Boston and Cleveland before giving specific instructions on the call. He informed the general, who was joined by Seward in Cleveland, that "the matter as far as possible" should be left in the hands of the governors, as the president wished. Buckingham received an enthusiastic response from all the governors he met. Border state Unionists, who had more to lose than Northern governors if rebels invaded their states, were miffed that Lincoln had failed to requisition volunteers from them. This slight was soon rectified, and on July 7, the border states' governors, Pierpont of Virginia, and Andrew Johnson, military governor of Tennessee, were included in the quotas "requested" by the president.[20]

The governors, except for Magoffin of Kentucky, whose Southern rights' views would soon cause him to resign under pressure from Unionists, assured Lincoln that they would attempt to meet their states' quotas for troops. (Governor Claiborne Jackson had been removed by the Missouri state convention in mid-1861 after he cast his lot with the Confederacy.) However, several of the governors admitted that it would be difficult to obtain volunteers for three-year terms or the duration of the war, which Lincoln wanted. Kirkwood of Iowa and Morton of Indiana informed Lincoln that their states would meet their quotas of men, but it could not be done immediately. A number of the governors advised the president and Stanton to reduce the period of enlistments for the new recruits.[21] Some recommended three-month enlistments; others wanted six-month terms. On July 3, Governor Israel Washburn Jr. of Maine telegraphed the president, "Recruiting for three years is terribly hard. Shall be obliged to resort to drafting unless I can be authorized to take volunteers for three or six months." On the same day, Lincoln, without mentioning the terms for the enlistments, wrote Washburn and the other governors, "I should not want the half of 300,000 if I could have them now. If I had 50,000 additional troops here now I believe I could substantially close the war in two weeks. But time is everything. . . . The quicker you send the fewer you will have to send."[22]

Still, despite the seriousness of the military situation, the governors found it increasingly hard to raise the troops Lincoln needed. Some again complained to the president and the War Department that they lacked the money to pay the necessary bonuses or bounties to the recruits; others, as in 1861, said that the call for troops interfered with the farming cycle. Strong political resistance to the war in the southern districts of Iowa, Illinois, Ohio, and Indiana bordering on Union slave states greatly hampered the work of recruitment officers. Peace advocates or Copperheads, centered in the revived Democratic Party and its press, opposed the war and began to challenge state and local Republican authority.[23] Women could be found in the opposition to enrollments in the army because the war "landed right in the center of their sphere, the family." Even in the East, serious opposition to recruitment developed. In Pennsylvania, a pamphlet circulated urging peace and the recognition of the Confederate States. Playing on the growing defeatism, Congressman Clement L. Vallandigham of Ohio emerged as the most famous or notorious leader of the Copperheads. His attacks on Lincoln and the war soon bordered on disloyalty.

Union officials and militia officers in the lower western states in 1862 began arresting opponents of the war and those who were discouraging recruitment in the army.[24] William A. Richardson, Illinois's most prominent Democrat, complained to Lincoln that twenty men, most of whom were influential citizens, had been arrested in his area alone.[25] The suppression of political dissent backfired on the Republicans, and it contributed to Democratic victories in the fall elections in Illinois and in other lower Northern states. Richardson himself was elected to the U.S. Senate by the new Illinois legislature.

With discontent rising, Governors Morton, Andrew, and Yates joined many Republicans in blaming the president and the War Department for their failure to win the war. Morton reproached Lincoln for his continued reluctance to act against secessionist sympathizers in Kentucky and expel rebel forces that had entered the Bluegrass State during the summer.[26] Andrew privately criticized the president for not including emancipation in the Union purpose of the war. He became upset when, on May 19, 1862, Lincoln revoked General David Hunter's abolition decree and his recruitment of blacks along the south Atlantic coast. The Massachusetts governor wrote to Secretary of War Stanton, "If our people feel that they are going into the South to help fight rebels, who will kill and destroy *them*," federal commanders should have the authority to "use [the] negro slaves against them, both as laborers and as fighting men." Andrew insisted that "if the President will . . . recognize *all* men, even black men, as legally capable of that loyalty the blacks are waiting to manifest, and let them fight . . . *the roads will swarm if need be with multitudes whom New England would pour out to obey*" the call for more troops and thereby regain the initiative in the war.[27]

Andrew still was unwilling during the grim spring and summer of 1862 to break his public silence and criticize Lincoln. However, he believed, as did his colleagues in other New England states, that the president was weak and under the cunning influence of Secretary of State Seward, whose prewar radicalism had turned toward conservatism during the war. Andrew told a friend that Lincoln could not maintain his proslavery border state policy much longer; he might be "slow," but soon he must defer to public demand for emancipation and the recruitment of black troops.[28]

Governor Yates criticized Lincoln directly and demanded harder blows in the war. On July 11, he telegraphed his old Illinois political associate, "[Your] conservative policy has utterly failed to reduce traitors to obedience and to restore the supremacy of the laws." Yates bluntly told the president, "The crisis of the war and our national existence is upon us. [It] demands greater efforts and sterner measures." The Illinois governor called for "greater animus and earnest [tactics]" to be "infused into our military movements; blows must be struck at the vital part of the Rebellion." Furthermore, the commanders, Yates wrote, meaning McClellan in the East and Don Carlos Buell in the Mississippi Valley, "should not be permitted to fritter away the sinews of our brave men in guarding the property of traitors and in driving back into their hands loyal blacks who offer us their labor & seek shelter [under] the federal flag."[29]

Yates did not specifically call for the freedom and arming of blacks; however, he must have known and approved of two bills before Congress that included emancipation and the military enlistment of the former slaves. The first bill, introduced by Senator Henry Wilson of Massachusetts, for a militia draft by the states, included the recruitment of blacks in the army and their freedom. The second bill, a new confiscation measure, would authorize the seizure of rebel property, free the slaves, and use them as soldiers or military laborers.[30] This bill, which was more stringent than the Confiscation Act of 1861, was opposed by border state governors and congressmen. Lincoln objected to the timing of the bill because it greatly complicated the border states' consideration of his gradual, compensated emancipation proposal. He also expressed certain constitutional reservations about the bill. Still, after Congress passed the measure on July 17, Lincoln signed it, though it proved virtually unenforceable.[31]

As in the case of the confiscation measure, a spirited debate raged in Congress over Senator Wilson's militia bill. Northern conservatives and Democrats joined border state members of Congress in blocking passage of the emancipation provision in the bill. The final bill authorized but did not require the president to enroll black troops. At this time, Lincoln opposed the enrollment of black people in the army because of the dangerous opposition it would encounter in the border states, an opposition led by the governors of these slave states.[32] However, he had no objection to their use as military laborers. By January 1, 1863, when he issued the Emancipation Proclamation, Lincoln had changed his mind and supported black recruitment in the army. He was motivated partly by the need to replace white troops killed and wounded on the bloody battlefields in the South during the last half of 1862.

Since he was not required to enroll black troops in the army, Lincoln on July 17, 1862, signed the militia bill, the same day that the confiscation measure became law. The Militia Act authorized the president to call the state militias into federal service for nine months to meet immediate troop needs in Virginia and elsewhere. It empowered the president to establish the rules for a militia draft.[33] The Militia Act, to be administered by the states and limited in its application, became the first step both toward national conscription and toward congressional approval for the recruitment of black troops in the army. Governor Andrew became the most active advocate of black recruitment.

Both the Second Confiscation Act and the Militia Act had been initiated independently of the president and were designed to some extent by the Republican majority in Congress to assert their authority in important matters of war policy. Actually, Lincoln was reluctant to get involved in congressional proceedings as well as the affairs of the governors. At Pittsburgh one month before he became president, Lincoln had announced, "My political education strongly inclines me against a very free use of any of [the] means by the Executive, to control the legislation of the country. As a rule, I think it better that the congress should originate, as well as perfect its measures, without external bias."[34] The debate on the militia bill during the summer of 1862, more so than on the confiscation bill, reflected Lincoln's prewar "political education" regarding the separation of federal powers and functions. Despite the growing need for greater executive involvement in federal legislation as the war progressed, Lincoln still rarely lobbied congressional members on issues or interfered with their work, though communication between the War Department and other federal departments and Congress increased.

With manpower needs mounting in the army, War Department officials went to work in late July drawing up directives for the militia draft. On August 4, Secretary of War Stanton, probably after consulting with the president, requisitioned three hundred thousand men "to serve for nine months unless sooner discharged." State quotas were established based on population. The draft, however, would apply to a state only if it failed to meet its quota of volunteers by August 15. As an incentive for the states to recruit three-year volunteers for the regiments, which the army obviously preferred to the nine-month men, the War Department ruled that each volunteer could count as four militiamen.[35] By meeting their quotas for three-year volunteers, the governors could avoid the militia draft, which their constituents bitterly resented, although state and local authorities would implement it.

On July 28, Lincoln, concerned about the uneven pace of recruitment of three-year volunteers, wrote to the governors urgently inquiring about the progress of enrollments. He wanted to know when the regiments would be ready.[36] William A. Buckingham of Connecticut gave a response that was echoed by several governors. He telegraphed Lincoln, "Recruiting for old regiments goes slowly; for new [regiments] everything looks promising." The governor reported that the first of these regiments would not be available for the federal army until September. The encampments, Buckingham told Lincoln, "are now delayed for want of supplies for which requisition was made early this month."[37] Recruitment of volunteers in the lower western states, and to a lesser extent in other states, faced strong resistance from Copperhead or peace elements and also because of the demands for agricultural labor. Some governors requested and secured postponement of the nine-month militia draft. In the end, only 87,588 men were furnished to the army under the Militia Act.[38]

Remarkably, in view of the growing casualties on the battlefield and opposition to recruitment, by the end of 1862 the governors and local officials, by extending bounties and other incentives, had enrolled 431,958 new and reenlisted volunteers.[39] Still, this figure was less than the number of volunteers and militiamen thought necessary to reverse the military setbacks of the summer and prevent the Confederate forces from taking the offensive in the war.

General McClellan's humiliating repulse around Richmond and serious Union military setbacks elsewhere had created a political crisis by late summer. Important state and congressional elections were scheduled for the fall; the war obviously would be the major issue in these contests. Faced with a deteriorating military and political situation, the president acted to breathe new life into the Union cause in the eastern theater, in Virginia. He replaced McClellan with John Pope, an aggressive general from the West who had the strong support of Governor Yates and other western governors.

Lincoln got more than he bargained for in the appointment of the rash and bombastic young general to command the army facing Lee. Instead of victories over "Bobby Lee," as Pope had promised, his aggressive tactics produced still another repulse and retreat for the Union army. On August 29–30, General Lee's Army of Northern Virginia routed Pope's Army of Virginia in the Second Battle of Bull Run, further demoralizing Unionists. With the morale of his army high, instead of marching on the federal capital as many expected, Lee chose to invade Maryland to "redeem" that slave state from Union control. He also hoped to move into Pennsylvania and seize its financial and material resources. Lee believed that if his campaign did not create political upheaval in the North and force Lincoln to abandon his aggression against the South, Great Britain and France would intervene and demand an end to the war, thereby ensuring Confederate independence.

At this critical juncture in the war, Lincoln, despite opposition from important members of his party, including those in his cabinet, restored McClellan to the command of a combined eastern army to resist Lee's invasion of Maryland. After all, Lincoln knew that McClellan was popular with his troops. The "Little Napoleon" also had the backing of border state Unionists and Northern Democrats, who approved of his support of their limited war aims. McClellan as well as the Democrats and border state conservatives wanted no tampering with slavery, the constitutional rights of the states, and the civil liberties of white people.

A meeting on September 6, 1862, of Lincoln and a delegation of three proslavery Kentucky Unionists provides an insight into border state and Northern Democratic support for McClellan. The delegation was sent by conservative governor James F. Robinson of Kentucky to discuss with the president the grim military situation that the nation and the Bluegrass State faced. Led by Garret Davis, a severe critic of Lincoln and the Republicans in the Senate, the Kentucky Unionists met with Lincoln four days after McClellan's reappointment to command. In a letter to the president immediately after the visit, the Kentuckians recalled their meeting with Lincoln, although they did not provide the details of the conversation. The president must have said what the Kentuckians wanted to hear, because in their letter to him they conveyed their "great satisfaction" with the meeting. They praised Lincoln for "the force, clearness, truth and *earnestness* with which [he] expressed [himself] in relation to the several points" raised in the interview. The Kentuckians told the president, "We believe that very small, if any, just exception can be taken to your policy in conducting the war to put down the rebellion."[40]

Senator Davis and the Kentucky Unionists in their letter to Lincoln specifically proclaimed their "unqualified approval" of his reappointment of McClellan to command the army confronting Lee. They indicated their "earnest hope that there [would be] no cause" to remove the general "or to interfere with him in his discharge of his duties." "We cannot doubt," they wrote, "that both, or either, would produce much evil to the army and the country." McClellan, the Kentuckians informed Lincoln, "certainly possesses a very large share of the confidence" of both the army and the country, "and you have given abundant proof that he has no less of yours."[41]

The Kentucky delegation did not mention emancipation as one of "the several points" raised in the meeting with the president. However, they probably discussed the matter and apparently were satisfied with Lincoln's response. The antislavery issue had become increasingly important—and contentious—during the summer, particularly after the border states rejected Lincoln's plan for compensated emancipation and Congress passed the Second Confiscation Act, authorizing the seizure of rebel slaves and other properties. Antislavery elements had increased their pressure on Lincoln to get at the roots of the rebellion, namely slavery.

The most publicized appeal for Lincoln to act forcibly to end slavery in the rebel states appeared in the *New York Tribune* on August 20, 1862, and was written by erstwhile radical editor Horace Greeley. In an article whose title, "The Prayer of Twenty Millions," exaggerated the support for emancipation in the Union states, Greeley insisted that the president enforce the Second Confiscation Act against the property of slaveholders and strike a major blow against the evil institution. Lincoln, who had given only tepid support to the new confiscation law, made an ambiguous response to Greeley's demand. The president famously wrote, "My paramount object in this struggle *is* to save the Union, and is *not* either to save or destroy slavery. If I could save the Union without freeing *any* slave I would do it, and if I could save it by freeing *all* the slaves I would do it; and if I could save it by freeing some and leaving others alone I would also do that. What I do about slavery, and the colored race, I do because I believe it helps to save the Union; and what I forbear, I forbear because I do *not* believe it would help to save the Union." The president's response to the New York editor suggested that the slavery issue was foremost in his mind.[42]

On September 13, one week after his conference with the Kentucky conservatives, Lincoln had a testy meeting with a delegation of Chicago Christian ministers who urged him to issue an emancipation proclamation. "What *good* would a proclamation of emancipation do," he asked, "especially as we are now situated" in the war? "I do not want to issue a document that the whole world will see must necessarily be inoperative, like the Pope's bull against the comet! Would *my word* free the slaves, when I cannot even enforce the Constitution in the rebel States?"[43]

Clearly, Lincoln had become irritated by the pressure on him regarding slavery. He confessed to the Chicago ministers that he was hammered on all sides by the issue. They argued that an antislavery proclamation, followed by the recruitment of black soldiers, would provide a principle around which to rally the free states in the war. Lincoln admitted that "slavery [was] the root of the rebellion, or at least [its] sine qua non," and that an emancipation proclamation could probably help the Union both in the North and in Europe. But, he contended, such a proclamation could turn over to the rebels "fifty thousand bayonets in the Union armies from the border Slave States." Lincoln chastised the Chicagoans for their failure to recognize that they already had "an important principle to rally and unite the people in the fact that constitutional government is at stake" in the war. "This is a fundamental idea, going about as deep as anything." The president ended the meeting in a conciliatory manner. "Do not misunderstand me," he told the ministers, "I have not decided against a proclamation of liberty to the slaves, but hold the matter under advisement. And I can assure you that the subject is on my mind, by day and night, more so than any other. Whatever shall appear to be God's will I will do."[44]

Meanwhile, Lincoln and Unionists everywhere hoped that McClellan could restore confidence to the Army of the Potomac and defeat Lee as he moved northward into Maryland. Many, however, including several governors, doubted that the "Little Napoleon" would succeed.

On September 4, two days after McClellan assumed command of the army, Lee's Confederate forces began crossing the Potomac at Leesburg, Virginia, south of Frederick, Maryland. Panic gripped Maryland and Pennsylvania, and concern spread into New Jersey and New York. Governor Curtin expressed the fears of his people when he frantically wrote to Lincoln that 190,000 rebels had invaded Maryland and were headed in the direction of Pennsylvania to "devastate & destroy" communities in their path. Another large force, Curtin reported, had concentrated in northern Virginia for the purpose of menacing Washington and keeping Union forces occupied while Lee's main army moved north.[45] Actually, Lee's invasion army consisted of only 50,000 men, far fewer than McClellan's 85,000 troops. Lincoln and the War Department had needlessly retained 72,500 men for the defense of Washington and vicinity.[46]

Curtin asked the president to endorse his militia call for all able-bodied men of Pennsylvania to repel the rebel forces. Lincoln gave approval to the governor's action. "I sanction the call that you have made," he informed Curtin, "and will receive them into the service and pay of the United States to the extent that they can be armed, equipped, and usefully employed." The federal government, Lincoln wrote, can provide arms only "for the quotas of militia furnished by the draft of nine-months' men, heretofore ordered." He believed, however, that the federal arms and "the 30,000 in your arsenal, will probably be sufficient for the purpose contemplated by your call."[47]

The Pennsylvania governor telegraphed Lincoln on the evening of September 11, asking the president to dispatch 80,000 "disciplined troops" to the state to resist the expected rebel invasion. The next morning, Lincoln replied that he did not have that many "disciplined troops" east of the mountains. Many of the new regiments, he informed Curtin, were with McClellan, "and close in the rear of the enemy supposed to be invading Pennsylvania." If he "start[ed] half of them to Harrisburg" as the governor wanted, Lincoln said, "the enemy will turn upon and beat the remaining half, and then reach Harrisburg before the part going there, and beat it too when it comes. The best possible security for Pennsylvania is putting the strongest [militia] force possible into the enemies [*sic*] rear."[48]

The governor acknowledged to Lincoln that his "reasons for not sending [the] force into Pennsylvania [was] entirely satisfactory." He assured the president, "We are doing all that is possible to throw forces into the Valley to check any movement the Rebels may attempt in this direction."[49] On September 14, Curtin reported to Lincoln, "We are massing forces quickly. Our people [are] responding to the call in a most wonderful manner."[50] Lee's army never invaded the Keystone State, at least in 1862, but it certainly was not clear at the time that it would not do so. The Confederate army was stopped in Maryland and forced to retreat back into Virginia. Curtin, whom historians have usually viewed as an undistinguished, passive leader who suffered from poor health, actually proved energetic in defending the state and capable as a war governor. He also was a valuable supporter of Lincoln's policies.

Meanwhile, in New York, the National War Committee of the city's prominent citizens urgently dispatched separately subcommittee members to visit the Northern governors and impress on them the seriousness of the situation. The committee also wanted to know how quickly the governors could forward troops to the front. On September 9, after returning to New York, the full subcommittee wrote a report to Lincoln on the efforts of the governors they had visited, which included those of the New England states, New York, New Jersey, Pennsylvania, and the three western states of Ohio, Indiana, and Illinois. The subcommittee informed Lincoln that most of the governors were sending troops forward as quickly as possible, despite encountering problems in recruitment and obtaining uniforms and equipment for the men. They provided the president with a somber finding regarding the mood in the western states: "It cannot be disguised that a wide spread disaffection with the conduct of the war exists at the West, and a change of measures imperatively demanded."[51]

The New York National War Committee also dispatched a deputation to visit the president for the purpose of urging a greater effort in the war. A reportedly happenstance meeting of five New England governors, while attending a college ceremony, occurred in Providence, Rhode Island. The governors, including John A. Andrew, suggested that when the New York delegation visited the White House, it should insist on the replacement of McClellan with General John C. Frémont. The New England governors also wanted the delegation to demand the removal of the wily William H. Seward and the conservative Montgomery Blair from the cabinet. They claimed that Seward and Blair's machinations had prevented the timid president from taking the necessary measures to defeat the rebels.[52]

On September 10, the New York delegation met with Lincoln, bringing with them the report of the committee members who had visited the governors. When the delegation demanded the reorganization of the cabinet, though without mentioning names, the president "became vexed," a member of the group reported. In rejecting their demand outright, Lincoln angrily told the New Yorkers, "It is plain enough what you want—you want to get Seward out of the Cabinet. There is not one of you who would not see the country ruined, if you could turn out Seward."[53]

After the meeting, Secretary of the Treasury Salmon P. Chase, the only true Radical Republican in the cabinet, made a point of talking to members of the New York delegation. He unfairly concluded from the meeting that the president had "yielded so much to Border State and negrophobin [sic] counsels that he now [found] it difficult to arrest his own descent towards the most fatal concessions." Chase then asked, "He has already separated himself from the great body of his party which elected him; distrusts those who most represents its spirit; and waits. For what?"[54] Chase sensed a Republican rebellion against Lincoln's leadership and hoped that Andrew and the New England governors would not be found wanting in the movement. The treasury secretary busied himself during September writing letters to political friends lamenting Lincoln's failures, while denying that he had any "personal complaint" against the president—a Chase tactic that became all too typical of him. Privately, he seemed to have believed that Lincoln had reneged on his promise, announced in confidence to his cabinet in July, to issue an emancipation proclamation.

The military situation for the Union in the Mississippi valley or western theater also had deteriorated since the successes of early 1862. During the summer, Confederate forces under Braxton Bragg and

Edmund Kirby Smith had invaded Kentucky and were on the march northward. At the same time as Lee's trouncing of General Pope at Bull Run, Smith's small army routed an inexperienced Union force at Richmond, Kentucky, and moved on toward Lexington. There, Senator Garret Davis and other prominent Unionists joined General Lew Wallace's troops in a futile defense of the town. Smith occupied Frankfort on September 3, chasing Governor James F. Robinson from the state capital. Only two weeks earlier, Robinson, a former Union Whig, had replaced the Democrat Beriah Magoffin in the office. From Frankfort, General Smith launched a raid toward Cincinnati while waiting for General Bragg to join him. Bragg was moving slowly and confidently through central Kentucky. In a humorous vein, which was unusual for him, Bragg jocularly announced, "My army has promised to make me military governor of Ohio."[55]

The Confederate campaign understandably produced panic not only among Kentucky Unionists but also among Ohioans and Indianans. Governor Tod rushed Ohio troops to Cincinnati to prevent an expected rebel assault on the city.[56] Demonstrating remarkable energy, Governor Morton of Indiana declared martial law in the state's river counties and dispatched reinforcements to Cincinnati, where General Wallace was establishing formidable defenses to withstand any Confederate attack. On September 11, General Smith's forces pushed within seven miles of Cincinnati; some of his troops reached Covington, Kentucky, on the Ohio River. However, they immediately withdrew, along with the main army, to the Lexington-Frankfort area, where Smith waited for Bragg.[57] The Confederate invasion of the Bluegrass State climaxed on October 8 at the Battle of Perryville in central Kentucky, followed by the withdrawal of Smith and Bragg to Tennessee. But Union success in the region was not secure. The possibility of another rebel penetration of Kentucky, supported by secessionists in the state, continued to worry the governors along the Ohio River. A bold raid in 1863 by rebel general John H. Morgan into southern Indiana and Ohio only reinforced their anxieties.

Even Missouri seemed in jeopardy of a major Confederate invasion during the late summer and fall of 1862. Although a Union army under General Samuel R. Curtis had defeated a rebel force in

March 1862 at Pea Ridge, across the Missouri border in Arkansas, few successes followed. Small Confederate armies returned to the southern part of Missouri during the summer, spawning brutal guerrilla attacks on Unionists and causing alarm. Bitter recriminations between provisional governor Hamilton Gamble and General Curtis, along with their subordinates, accompanied these Union setbacks. The quarrels between the civil and military leaders in the state angered Lincoln when he had to intervene, though without much success. The Confederates remained in the state until repulsed at Springfield, Missouri, in January 1863.[58]

The old conflict on the Missouri-Kansas border between pro-slavery Missourians and antislavery Kansans intensified in 1862. Vengeance and plunder, however, seemed to be the main motives for the attacks. In September, Missouri governor Gamble excitedly reported to Lincoln that he feared an invasion of the western counties by Kansas Jayhawkers, including "organizations of negroes . . . armed and equipped as soldiers of the United States, for the purpose of entering this state and committing depredations."[59] Tragically, the border conflict became a cruel civil war within a civil war, which Lincoln and the War Department did not have the military means to quell. To make matters worse for the president, in Minnesota a sudden Indian uprising occurred in August, which diverted the attention of the governors of Iowa and Wisconsin, as well as Governor Ramsey of Minnesota, away from the war in the South.

By mid-September 1862, the Union cause in the Civil War had reached its nadir, and federal emancipation seemed only a remote possibility. The course of the war deeply troubled Lincoln and the governors in the Union states, including the border slave states. They especially worried about what effect the fall elections would have on the Union cause.

.

THE ALTOONA CONFERENCE

O n September 10, 1862, Radical Republican senator Zacha-
riah Chandler of Michigan wrote to his colleague Lyman
Trumbull of Illinois, "Nothing will now save us but a demand
of the loyal governors, *backed by a threat*, that a change of policy
and men shall instantly be made."[1] A few days earlier, Governor
Curtin of Pennsylvania sensed the need for the governors to confer
and adopt a strong statement backing the war and strengthening
the hand of the government. On September 6, Curtin telegraphed
Governor Andrew of Massachusetts, "In the present emergency
would it not be well that the Loyal Governors should meet at some
point in the border states to take measures for the active support of
the government."[2]

On the same day, Andrew replied to Curtin that he would gladly
attend such a meeting. Curtin sent a similar message to several other
governors. Encouraged by their positive responses, on September 14
the Pennsylvania governor issued a formal invitation for the state
executives to meet at Altoona in his state on the twenty-fourth. He
added the names of David Tod of Ohio and Francis H. Pierpont of
the Restored (Union) Government of Virginia to the call.[3] Pierpont's
constituency was mainly in western Virginia, which then was in the
process of forming the state of West Virginia. His Virginia government had been recognized by both the president and Congress, and
the rump Union legislature had approved of the separation of the
western counties to form the new state.

By placing Tod and Pierpont's names on the call for the Altoona conference, Curtin, a middle-of-the-road Republican, hoped to avoid criticism that the meeting was designed to advance a radical New England agenda. The ploy did not work. The invitation to the governors had hardly cleared the telegraph wires in the state capitals when border state conservatives and Northern Democrats charged that Andrew and other New England governors had planned the meeting to attack the president, demand the reorganization of the cabinet, and secure the ouster of General McClellan in favor of General Frémont, who had been the 1856 Republican candidate for president. They believed the New Englanders had concluded that, unlike McClellan, if Frémont were commander of the Army of the Potomac, he would conduct a hard war to save the Union and end slavery. Conservatives claimed that the New England Radicals, led by Andrew, planned nothing less than a coup against the government.

The intentions of Andrew and like-minded Radicals were not as extreme as the conservatives charged. Although the Massachusetts governor had come out boldly for emancipation in August 1862, by this time it was hardly a radical proposal as a war measure. Andrew declared that the war could not and should not end until the "dreadful iniquity" of slavery had been "trodden beneath [their] feet."[4] Instead of wanting to replace Lincoln, however, Andrew wrote to a friend that he sought "to save the Pres[iden]t. from the infamy of ruining his country."[5]

At Altoona, Andrew and other New England governors, like their counterparts elsewhere, wanted to avoid a divisive confrontation over the president and the conduct of the war, which could further undermine the Union effort to suppress the rebellion. They hoped, however, that Lincoln would see the wisdom of acting against slavery in the rebel states, which the Second Confiscation Act in July had authorized him to do, but he had virtually ignored this new power. Governor William A. Buckingham of Connecticut, though he failed to arrive in time to participate in the Altoona conference, had made this point clear to the president when he and a delegation from his state met in August with Lincoln at the White House. They were taken aback by Lincoln's immediate response to their suggestion that he issue a proclamation freeing the slaves in the rebel states. "I suppose," he said, "what your people want is more nigger" in Connecticut.[6]

Despite his Indiana and Illinois background, in which the use of the n-word, even by antislavery men, was common, Lincoln rarely expressed such racist epithets. In the meeting with Buckingham and his delegation, the president's racist comment reflected his own inner struggle to act in a constitutional manner against slavery as antislavery pressure mounted on him during the summer. On the other hand, conservatives repeatedly warned him against changing the original Union purpose of the war. Sensing the disapproval of the Connecticut delegation, Lincoln's tone in his meeting with them quickly softened. He told his visitors that he had been doing his utmost to remove the main cause of the war—slavery—and end the republic's shame and curse. The president, according to Buckingham, acknowledged that he had "registered a vow in heaven to free" the slaves of rebels after a major battle was won.[7]

Although they did not want to create a public row at Altoona, several of the governors came prepared to argue for changes in the administration's war policies and military leadership. Western governors Yates, Kirkwood, and Morton now agreed with the New Englanders that emancipation should be used as a military tool to win the war. Although Yates had vigorously supported Lincoln for president in 1860, he expressed his disappointment with the president's leadership and wanted changes in the conduct of the war and the army commanders. Soon after the Altoona conference, Yates admitted to a Brooklyn audience, "Old Abe was too slow for me. I was for [an emancipation] proclamation, for confiscation, for conscription, for the arrest of rebels and traitors, and for every measure by which we could put down the rebellion."[8] Kirkwood and Morton wanted the Altoona conference to seek McClellan's removal from command of the Army of the Potomac and place greater emphasis on the war in the West. Morton was facing a growing Copperhead threat, and though supportive of the meeting, he said he was too busy with military and political matters to leave Indiana and go to Altoona; instead, he sent a representative. Yates and Kirkwood attended the conference.[9]

An Indian uprising in Minnesota beginning in August prevented Governor Alexander Ramsey from participating in the Altoona conference. The governor of a still largely frontier state, Ramsey's overwhelming concern was protecting white settlers, and he had little time for the war in the South. On September 6, Ramsey frantically telegraphed Lincoln that more than five hundred whites had been "murdered" by Dakota Sioux Indians, and Minnesota needed immediate federal help to suppress the uprising. "This is not our war," he told the president, "it is a National War." The governor urged Lincoln to "direct the purchase or send five hundred horses or order the Minnesota Companies of horse in Kentucky and Tennessee home. Answer me at once," he demanded."[10]

Instead, Lincoln dispatched the recently discredited General John Pope to Minnesota to assist General Henry H. Sibley, who commanded the state militia, directing Pope to assume control of all the forces in the state. Upon arriving in Saint Paul on September 16, Pope telegraphed General Henry W. Halleck in the War Department that he found "panic everywhere in Wisconsin and Minnesota." He informed Halleck, "We are likely to have a general Indian war all along the frontier, unless immediate steps are taken to put a stop to it." Already, "terrible destruction" had occurred in the state. Pope asked Governor Edward Salomon of Wisconsin to send three or four regiments to Minnesota to aid against the Dakota Sioux. He frankly acknowledged that his purpose was "to exterminate the Sioux if [he had] the power to do so." Operating from Saint Paul, Pope, who earlier had bragged that his headquarters was in the saddle, instructed General Sibley to treat the Dakota Sioux "as maniacs or wild beasts, and by no means as people with whom treaties or compromises can be made."[11] Sibley agreed with Pope. Even Governor Ramsey urged a merciless policy against the Sioux.

Meanwhile, Governor Tod of Ohio, concerned that the Indian uprising would hurt the war against the South, recommended to Secretary of War Stanton that paroled Union prisoners at Annapolis be sent to the Minnesota frontier. Both Stanton and Lincoln thought the idea was "excellent." The president directed that these men, numbering about twenty thousand, be dispatched to the state immediately.

They refused to go, however, and Lincoln finally agreed that it would violate their parole to force them to go west and fight the Indians.[12]

By mid-October 1862, the insurrection had been crushed. At least 450 and perhaps as many as 1,000 white settlers and soldiers had been killed; the number of Dakota Sioux casualties is unknown. White Minnesotans demanded quick and severe justice for the captured Indian "fiends." A military commission sentenced 303 Dakotas to death, verdicts that required the president's approval. Lincoln carefully pared down the number of insurgents to 38 for execution. In December, they were hanged at Mankato, Minnesota, in the largest public execution in American history. The other prisoners were transported outside the state, and those who survived were eventually freed.[13] After the 1864 presidential contest, Ramsey visited the White House and talked about the election. Lincoln commented that he had won Minnesota by seven thousand votes, compared with ten thousand four years earlier. "If he had hung more Indians," Ramsey said, "we should have given him his old majority," a remark that rightly offended the president. "I could not afford to hang men for votes," Lincoln declared.[14]

In February and March 1863, Congress voided all treaties with the Dakota Sioux and Winnebago in Minnesota and ordered their removal from the state. Republican senator Morton Wilkinson of Minnesota, who sponsored the bill, argued that "humanity requires [removal]; the welfare of the Indians as well as the peace of the whites demand it."[15] Few Minnesotans objected to the expulsion. Even Henry B. Whipple, the state's Protestant Episcopal bishop, who visited the president to call for an end to the corrupt federal Indian system, endorsed the action on the shallow ground that it would separate the Indians from evil white influences. Lincoln did nothing to prevent the removal, though he might have been troubled by it. He reportedly remarked to Whipple, "If we get through this war" in the South, "and I live, *this Indian system shall be reformed.*"[16]

Governor Ramsey rode his reputation as a defender of the state against the Dakota Sioux "assassins" and "ravishers" of women to a U.S. Senate seat in 1863. Ironically, in the Senate, Ramsey affiliated with the Radical Republicans and became a supporter of black rights in the South.

In neighboring Wisconsin, Governor Salomon feared that the "Minnesota troubles" would inspire a similar uprising of Winnebago in the interior of his state. Although he attended the Altoona conference on September 24, 1862, Salomon's main concern at this time was the defense of the frontier. This German American governor called on the War Department for weapons to arm his citizens against the expected Indian attacks. "The call is urgent," he wired Secretary of War Stanton on September 2. "Appeals are daily made to me for arms and ammunition." Receiving no response, he telegraphed Stanton again on September 5. "I am positively advised of the presence of emissaries" among the Winnebago "from other tribes," he wrote, "and there is good reason to believe these emissaries to be in the interest of the [Southern?] rebels on Lake Superior." The governor was quick to chastise Stanton for his failure to send the arms, declaring, "Your delays are cruel."[17]

Realizing that no Indian outbreak had actually occurred in Wisconsin, Stanton, after conferring with Lincoln, telegraphed a brusque reply to Salomon's excited appeal: "You are entirely mistaken in supposing that you are the exclusive judge as to whether arms and ammunition of the General Government are to be sent to your State. The President must be the judge. You have not until now stated any fact for the judgment of the President" to act on, "but contented yourself with giving imperious orders."[18] As might be expected, Salomon shot back, "The tone of your last dispatch is entirely unjustifiable" and reminded Stanton that the War Department "has charge of the Indians, and should know there are thousands" of them in Wisconsin. He told the secretary of war, "I do not propose to wait until the butchery commences, as in Minnesota," before arming the people with whatever weapons they could obtain. Before leaving for the Altoona conference, the governor issued a not-so-subtle threat to withhold the state's quota of troops to fight the rebels in the South if Stanton did not honor his request for arms.[19]

The Indian war in Minnesota also threatened to spill over into Iowa, a state with about seven hundred thousand white people. On September 8, Governor Kirkwood telegraphed Stanton that the danger of a Yankton Indian uprising on the state's northwestern border with Minnesota and the Dakota Territory was "imminent, and nothing but prompt action can stop the terrible massacre." "The settlers are fleeing by [the] hundreds," Kirkwood reported to Stanton. He requested that two regiments, equipped for service in the South, be sent immediately to the region and placed under the command of General William S. Harney, a veteran Indian fighter. Kirkwood had exaggerated the threat to the area. Although a few minor incidents occurred on the state's border with the Dakota Territory, Iowa Frontier Rangers prevented any serious Indian outbreak.[20]

Kirkwood, like Governor Salomon, also participated in the governors' conference in Pennsylvania. Apparently neither governor raised the issue of frontier security at Altoona. Republican governor Charles Robinson of Kansas had his hands full at home with rebel guerrillas on his state's border with Missouri and did not go to Altoona.

Border slave state governors, who faced Confederate invasions at home, suspected that the Radical Republican governors would dominate the Altoona meeting and endorse the abolition of slavery and recruitment of black troops in the army. They believed that Lincoln, as a result of the conference, would succumb to the pressure of Northern governors like Andrew and adopt an antislavery agenda. Therefore, Governors William Burton of Delaware, James F. Robinson of Kentucky, and Hamilton R. Gamble of Missouri refused to participate in the meeting. Gamble's brother-in-law, U.S. attorney general Edward Bates, warned him not to go to Altoona because "whatever [its] design, the end is revolutionary," and it would be controlled by the extreme wing of the Republican Party.[21] On the other hand, Augustus W. Bradford of Maryland, despite his suspicions regarding the Radicals' purposes, believed that the meeting was too important to miss given that his state had become a battleground of the war. He accepted the invitation to join the other governors at Altoona.

Democratic governor Charles S. Olden of New Jersey, though a strong supporter of the war, also was concerned that the Radicals might prevail in Altoona and adopt resolutions that would undermine his position at home. Nevertheless, he attended the conference. Governor Edwin D. Morgan, the conservative Republican governor of New York, feared that the adoption of a radical agenda would hurt his wing of the party with the approach of a bitterly contested election in the state. He remained at home, explaining to Curtin, "My first duty is to raise and forward the six hundred thousand men required by the Government, until after which I shall not be able to leave these Headquarters."[22]

On September 24, 1862, two days after Lincoln issued his preliminary Emancipation Proclamation, eleven Union governors and a representative of Governor Morton of Indiana assembled at the Logan House in Altoona, Pennsylvania. Governor Curtin chose this site for the conference because the town had good railroad connections to both the East and West, and the Logan House was reputedly the finest hotel between Harrisburg and Pittsburgh. Governor Austin Blair of Michigan arrived too late to participate in the meeting; however, he joined the other governors when they visited Lincoln on the twenty-sixth and presented him with the resolutions adopted at Altoona.

Before the governors began their talks in one of the hotel's three plush parlors, dramatic events had occurred in the war. On September 17, General McClellan repulsed General Lee's Confederate forces in the bloody one-day Battle of Antietam near Sharpsburg, Maryland. After the battle, Lee began a retreat back to and across the Potomac, with McClellan in a slow, unsuccessful pursuit.

Despite Lincoln's bitter disappointment that the rebel army had escaped destruction in Maryland, McClellan's "victory" at Antietam provided the president the opportune moment to issue his preliminary Emancipation Proclamation. He had earlier told his cabinet that he would announce the proclamation after a military success but subsequently experienced indecision about it. Issued on September 22, the proclamation promised freedom to slaves in any rebel state or congressional district, beginning on January 1, if it had not renewed its allegiance to the Union. Most of the governors learned of the proclamation on the train en route to Altoona.[23] Although historians have assumed that the president issued the proclamation with the governors' conference in mind and in order to undercut the Radicals in his party on emancipation, Lincoln later told Congressman George S. Boutwell of Massachusetts, "I never thought of the meeting of the governors at Altoona, and I can hardly remember that I knew anything about it."[24] Lincoln's proclamation, however, became an important subject of discussion when the governors met on September 24. Its announcement two days earlier probably forestalled a divisive debate on emancipation at Altoona.

Curtin, Tod, and other middle-of-the road governors, while agreeing or acquiescing on federal emancipation for the rebel states, gained control of the meeting. They quickly moved to quash rumors that the governors planned an anti-Lincoln coup by securing the selection of Augustus W. Bradford, the conservative proslavery governor of Maryland, to preside over the session. The governors agreed that the discussions should be confidential and that, except for a final "address" to the president, no record of the proceedings should be kept. However, Governor Kirkwood later reported that a number of issues were discussed in addition to Lincoln's preliminary Emancipation Proclamation. These included McClellan's fitness for command and the reorganization of the president's cabinet.[25] Governor Andrew reportedly argued for an hour on the need for a stronger statement on ending slavery than Lincoln's Emancipation Proclamation. He wanted the president to free all slaves in the South, including those in the border states, and also order the recruitment of black troops in the army. However, the Massachusetts governor received little support for what was viewed in 1862 as a radical position, and he ultimately acquiesced in the majority's position that the president's proclamation was adequate. Partly in order to placate him, Andrew was asked to write, with Curtin's assistance, the approved resolutions or address of the governors to the president.[26]

In the address, the governors, except for Bradford, "hail[ed] with heartfelt gratitude" the president's proclamation "declaring [slaves] emancipated from their bondage . . . in the rebel States." They insisted that for the government "to have continued indefinitely the most efficient cause, support and stay of the rebellion"—slavery—"would have been . . . unjust to the loyal people whose treasures and lives are made a willing sacrifice on the altar of patriotism." The governors maintained that "the right to establish martial or military govern-ment in a State or Territory in rebellion," which they implied that Lincoln had done, confirmed "the duty of the Government to liberate the minds of all men living therein [with] assurances of protection, in order that all who are capable, intellectually and morally, of loyalty and obedience, may not be forced into treason as the unwilling tools of rebellious traitors." They predicted, "The decision of the President to strike at the root of the rebellion," again referring to slavery, "will lend new vigor to the [Union] efforts and new life and hope to the hearts of the people." His antislavery policy "will be crowned with success, will give speedy and triumphant victories over our enemies, and secure to this Nation and this people the blessing and favor of Almighty God."[27]

Although the Emancipation Proclamation would be limited to the states still in rebellion on January 1, the governors at Altoona hoped that it would mark the beginning of the end of slavery in America. The possibility that any of those states would cease their rebellion and voluntarily return to the Union by that date, however, was remote. Lincoln ultimately excluded two congressional districts in the New Orleans area and two districts in Virginia from the application of the final proclamation because, as he had promised in the preliminary document, they were controlled by Unionists. After military governor Andrew Johnson and other Tennessee loyalists complained that the proclamation would damage the Union cause in their state, Lincoln exempted all of Tennessee from it, even though the eastern area, where most Unionists lived, was under rebel control.

Governor Andrew informed a friend that Lincoln's proclamation was "a *poor* document, but a mighty *act*; slow, somewhat halting, wrong in its delay till January, but grand and sublime after all."[28] Despite its faults, Andrew wrote, "our Republicans must make it *their* business to sustain this act of Lincoln, and we will drive the 'conservatism'" of the proslavery forces "and the reactionaries of des-potism into the very caves and holes of the Earth." He confidently predicted that "the conquest of the rebels, the emancipation of the slaves, and the restoration of peace founded on liberty and permanent democratic ideas" would then occur.[29]

The lower North governors, with the approach of important fall elections in their politically divided states, sought to avoid drawing too much attention to Lincoln's proclamation. Curtin, though he supported emancipation, expressed his fear that the proclamation would lose Pennsylvania to the Democrats in the elections.[30] In the governors' address to the president, after endorsing emancipation, they avoided the inflammatory issues of slavery in the border states, the rights of black people after freedom, and black troops in the army.

The only serious disagreement at Altoona involved the continuation of General McClellan as commander of the Army of the Potomac. Much to the disappointment of the governors, as well as Lincoln, the general failed to follow up on his success at Antietam and crush Lee's army. The governors correctly concluded that the "Young Napoleon" still had a case of the "slows." However, Curtin and Bradford, whose states had been saved from the Confederates and who wanted to believe that McClellan would soon confront and defeat Lee, defended the general in the meeting. They were joined by Governor Tod, who remembered that McClellan had earlier cleared western Virginia and the Ohio valley of rebels. In the Altoona conference, Andrew, Yates, and Kirkwood angrily attacked McClellan. The Massachusetts governor reportedly proposed that an excellent choice to replace McClellan would be Frémont, the hero of the Radical Republicans for issuing his proclamation to free slaves in Missouri in 1861, only to have it revoked by Lincoln.

Some of the governors must have been amused by the Frémont suggestion, as he had proved his unworthiness as a military commander in Missouri. In the end, the opponents of McClellan agreed with the other governors not to air publicly their criticisms of the general in their address to the president. Expressing their lack of confidence in McClellan in a public statement, which the address was certain to become, would have undermined the spirit of unity and support for the war that the governors sought at Altoona. The governors did agree to raise privately their strong objections to McClellan when they met with Lincoln after the conference.[31]

The governors' address also avoided any mention of their unhappiness with other generals, specifically Don Carlos Buell, commanding in the Mississippi valley, or with members of Lincoln's cabinet. Like political leaders in other wars, the governors praised the soldiers for their "splendid valor, their patient endurance, their manly patriotism, and their devotion to duty." Importantly, they pledged "to surround the President with [their] constant support, trusting that the fidelity and zeal of the loyal States and people will always assure him that he will be constantly maintained in pursuing with the utmost vigor this war for the preservation of the national life and the hope of humanity." The governors promised to carry out all "the lawful orders of the President, co-operating always in [their] spheres with the National Government," and provide "the most vigorous exercise of all [their] lawful and proper powers" to suppress the rebellion. They also "respectfully asked" Lincoln to call for a reserve "force of volunteers for one-year's service, of not less than 100,000" men, the requisitions for each state "to be raised after it filled its quota" of volunteers and militia troops. The military reserves, according to the governors, should be "constantly kept on foot, to be raised, armed, equipped, and trained at home, and ready for emergencies" when needed.[32]

Lincoln could not have asked for more from the Union governors at Altoona. They had supported his conduct of the war, avoided a public attack on the cabinet and General McClellan, and endorsed the president's Emancipation Proclamation. Their support for the establishment of martial law reinforced Lincoln's proclamation on the same day as the Altoona conference suspending the writ of habeas corpus for "all Rebels and Insurgents, their aiders and abettors within the United States, and all persons discouraging voluntary enlistments, resisting militia drafts, or guilty of any disloyal practice." The president declared that violators, even in the Northern states, would "be subject to martial law and liable to trial and punishment by Courts Martial or Military Commission." This sweeping proclamation opened the door to a barrage of criticism from Democrats and conservatives, who had good reason to fear for their civil liberties in the hands of overzealous military commanders.[33] The governors' approval of the president's action, however, defused some of the criticism hurled his way for his suspension of the writ of habeas corpus and the antislavery proclamation, particularly among conservative members of his party and some Democrats. Although the governors recommended that Lincoln issue a call for a reserve force of one hundred thousand, he did not ask for these troops at this time.

Governor Curtin later recalled that his colleagues at Altoona had been careful in the address to avoid anything that might embarrass the administration or challenge the president's authority and management of the war. Such criticisms, the governors knew, would have contributed to further divisions in the Union states and demoralized the army. The governors' intentions were to provide moral support for a vigorous prosecution of the war and for the sacrifices, including the expansion of military forces, still needed to win the war.

At the end of the one-day conference, the Union governors, as agreed, went to Washington to deliver their address to the president. They also wanted to express in person and in secret their concerns, which they had discussed at Altoona but would have been damaging to reveal publicly. On September 26, they met with the president in the White House.[34] Lincoln agreed with the governors that their discussion should be confidential. A *New York Tribune* correspondent was denied admission to the meeting room when he appeared at the door. The lack of openness inevitably heightened suspicions about the purposes of the governors, especially among Northern Democrats and border state conservatives. The popular *New York Herald* lent support to these suspicions when it concluded that from the beginning, the Altoona meeting had been "a vast conspiracy . . . set on foot by the radicals . . . to depose the present administration and place Frémont at the head of a provisional government."[35]

Even Secretary of the Navy Gideon Welles had concerns about the conference and the governors' visit with the president. On the day of the meeting with Lincoln, Welles recorded in his diary, "The Governors of the loyal States called to-day on the President. They have had a meeting at Altoona, for what purpose I scarcely know. It was an unauthorized gathering of State Executives, doubtless with good intent; but I dislike these irregular and extraordinary movements. They must tend to good or evil, and I see no good. These officials had better limit their efforts within their legitimate sphere."[36]

Governor Andrew opened the White House meeting by reading the Altoona address to the president. The document had been signed by eleven governors, including Blair of Michigan, who had missed the Altoona conference, and by Governor Morton's representative. After Andrew had finished, the president "made a very short & pleasant reply to the address," Blair later wrote.[37] Lincoln thanked the governors for all they had done and for their promise "to help the General Government in this great crisis." He told the group that "no fact had assured him so thoroughly of the justice" of the Emancipation Proclamation than the governors' "hearty approbation." Lincoln informed them that, "as to the suggestions which they had made in [their] address, he was grateful for them all, but at that moment he would not answer them specifically." However, he "believed that he should carry most if not all of them out, so far as possible."[38] Because the president approved the points in the address, and also would later talk to the governors individually, he saw no need to write a formal response to the document.

A general discussion of the war followed Lincoln's brief statement. The talks quickly turned to an evaluation of General McClellan's performance as the commander of the Army of the Potomac. Several governors criticized the general, with Governor Kirkwood of Iowa the most outspoken. Kirkwood rose from his seat and, in frank language, addressed the president. Years after the meeting, he vividly recalled telling the president that he spoke for the people of Iowa when he said that McClellan had demonstrated his incapacity for command. The governor argued that, though the western armies had won most of the Union victories in the war, McClellan's army, which "was better and sooner armed, better clothed, better equipped in every way," had not succeeded. "Our western troops," Kirkwood declared, "were always doing something and McClellan was only getting ready" to fight, despite the bravery of his men.[39]

At this point, Lincoln quipped, "You Iowa people then judge generals as you do lawyers, by their success in trying cases." Not to be outdone, Kirkwood shot back, "Yes, something like that; the lawyer who is always losing his cases, especially when he was right and had justice on his side don't get much practice in Iowa." After further comment, Kirkwood bluntly declared, "Mr. President, our Iowa people fear and I fear that the Administration is afraid to remove Gen. McClellan." Color came to Lincoln's face, and Kirkwood, according to his account, immediately felt that he had blundered. In a different tone, the governor explained that Iowans believed that McClellan "and his toadies in the army," along with "a certain class of politicians outside the army," had made successful efforts "to attach his soldiers to him personally." They had caused "his soldiers to believe that the severe criticisms to which the General has been subjected are intended to apply to them . . . as well as to him." The minds of the soldiers, Kirkwood claimed, "have so prejudiced" them in favor of McClellan "as to make it unsafe to remove him for fear his removal might cause insubordination, perhaps mutiny; that is what I meant when I spoke of your being afraid to remove him." The president remained silent for a moment, "and then he said slowly and with emphasis, 'Gov. Kirkwood, if I believed our cause be benefitted by removing Gen. McClellan to-morrow, I would remove him to-morrow, and not till then.'"[40]

Lincoln further took Kirkwood's remarks to mean that McClellan's loyalty was in question. As Governor Blair of Michigan remembered, the president angrily responded, "Do I believe in the loyalty of Gen. McClellan? Of course I believe in his loyalty. I have the same reasons to believe in his loyalty that I have to believe in the loyalty of you gentlemen before me. I cannot dive into the hearts of men and find what is there." Lincoln paused for a moment, and then carefully announced in a revealing commentary on the general, "After having said so much in favor of Gen. McClellan, I don't want you [to] think that I do not know his deficiencies. . . . He is over cautious and lacking in confidence in himself & in his ability to win victories with the forces at his command. He fights a battle about as well as any of them when he does fight, but when a substantial victory is won"—Lincoln clearly had Antietam in mind—"he seems incapable of properly following it up so as to reap the fruits of it, and it does not seem to do us any good. But if I remove him some one must be put in his place. Who shall it be?" Governor Blair asked, "Why not try another man Mr. President?" Whereupon Lincoln replied,

"Ah: but I might lose an army by that," which suggested that he also was concerned about the reaction of McClellan's troops and supporters outside the army if he removed the general.[41]

The meeting ended on a friendly note; even Kirkwood expressed his satisfaction with Lincoln's responses to the governors' Altoona address.[42] Governor Tod, who had defended the general during the discussion, reported to Secretary of the Navy Welles after the meeting that "his confidence in McClellan is unimpaired, and in the President it is greatly increased." Tod now had "full, unwavering confidence the country will be extricated and the Union maintained."[43]

Because only about half of the Union governors had attended the conference and signed the address, Lincoln sought the approval of the others. He understood that the document's endorsement of emancipation would preclude the border state governors from signing the address, except perhaps for Governor Bradford of Maryland. Lincoln believed that if he could persuade Bradford to agree to the address, it would allay conservative concerns regarding his policies. In an effort to obtain the Maryland governor's approval, Lincoln gave Bradford's wife a pass to visit her rebel son in Virginia.[44]

The ploy did not work; Bradford still refused to sign the address. However, Governor Pierpont of the rump Union government of Virginia, who depended on Lincoln's support and whose wife was antislavery, readily endorsed the document. In the end, Lincoln secured the agreement of all the Union governors except for those of the four border states, as well as Democrat Charles S. Olden of New Jersey and Republican Edwin Morgan of New York. Morgan weakly explained that he could not approve "the proceedings of a meeting at which [he] was not present."[45] In declining to sign the address, Hamilton Gamble of Missouri expressed the view of border state governors when he wrote that the document was an unwarranted interference with state authority. He mainly meant this in regard to slavery. On the other hand, military governor Andrew Johnson of Tennessee endorsed the address, though he later secured his state's exemption from the Emancipation Proclamation. Like Pierpont, Johnson had been appointed by Lincoln to restore his state to the Union, and he depended on the president's backing for his reconstruction efforts.[46]

The newspapers immediately published the governors' address to the president. Republican newspapers and some Democratic sheets praised it and said that the work of the Altoona conference would strengthen support for the war. Both the Democratic *Boston Herald* and the old Whig *Washington National Intelligencer* concluded that the address was a conservative document, despite its endorsement of the Emancipation Proclamation.[47] Nonetheless, a number of Democratic newspapers and leaders had little use for the address, especially its support of emancipation and martial law. They immediately attached conspiratorial motives to the governors' meeting. The *New York Herald* characterized the Altoona conference as a meeting of the "Disloyal Governors of the Loyal States" and labeled it "A Second Hartford Convention" designed to replace Lincoln with the radical John C. Frémont.[48]

William O. Stoddard, a presidential secretary, sought to refute the conspiracy rumors about the governors' meeting at Altoona and with the president. In a dispatch to the *New York Examiner* several days after the conference, Stoddard reported that while the governors met with Lincoln, "the quid-nuncs of the press wandered through hotel passages, applied their ears to numberless keyholes, peered through aggravating curtained windows, snuffing treason, seeing ghosts of Frémont, and transforming a squad of patriotic gentlemen" or governors "into a gang of [Roman] Catilines plotting the ruin of—McClellan." Stoddard exaggerated when he claimed, "Never was anything more cordial and harmonious than the meeting of the President and his gubernatorial guests." He was correct, however, when he wrote that at their parting, "nothing could have been more full of good-will and mutual promises of active cooperation."[49]

Even in Massachusetts, Governor Andrew had to defend himself from criticism of his role in the Altoona conference. Professor Joel Parker of the Harvard Law School, an ultraconservative who sought to block Andrew's renomination by state Republicans, charged that the governor had conspired against the president at Altoona. Parker, an old Whig who believed that the Emancipation Proclamation was unconstitutional, announced that Andrew had forced Lincoln to issue the proclamation the day before the governor's met.[50] This was not true. Andrew had learned of the proclamation only while en route to Altoona; the news came as a pleasant surprise to him. However, had the president not issued the proclamation before the conference, Andrew, backed by the New England governors and perhaps by Richard Yates of Illinois, could have turned the meeting into a divisive attack on Lincoln for his failure to act against slavery and his war leadership. The radical governors conceivably could have faulted the president for his inability to suppress the rebellion, his support of McClellan, and his appeasement of the border states.

Parker also claimed that Andrew at Altoona had plotted to gain control of Lincoln and advance a radical agenda. In response, the governor reminded New Englanders that it was "the conservative governors who summoned us to Altoona." Andrew insisted that he had attended the conference solely for the purpose of "helping to strengthen the arm of the President" and the military forces. At Altoona, he had called only for the ouster of McClellan, though he wanted Secretary of State William H. Seward and Postmaster General Montgomery Blair, both viewed as evil geniuses behind the president, replaced in the cabinet. In the end, Andrew won the Republican Party's renomination for governor of Massachusetts, and in the election, he defeated the "People's Party" candidate endorsed by Parker and the Democrats.

Coming at a dark time in the war when Union morale had reached a low point, the Altoona conference provided a needed boost to public support for the military effort against the rebellion. Governor Austin Blair of Michigan later wrote that the publication of the Altoona address "at once made known to the people the vigorous policy recommended by the Governors, [and] it had some influence in restoring confidence in the ability of the government to sustain itself" and suppress the rebellion. The governors' support of the Lincoln administration and the war, according to Blair, "promoted enlistments in the states, and infused greater activity into the recruiting service, [thereby] strengthen[ing] the armies in the field."[51] Even the demanding secretary of war Stanton, in his annual report in December 1862, acknowledged the yeoman work of the governors, notably their roles in meeting the president's two calls for troops during the summer. Stanton announced, however, that the time had come for Congress to give the federal government the main responsibility for raising troops.[52] A major step in this direction occurred when Congress approved the Enrollment Act and the president signed it on March 3, 1863, ushering in national military conscription. It became the most controversial and divisive law enacted during the Civil War.

Governor Blair claimed that the Emancipation Proclamation, praised by the governors in their address to the president, aided the Union cause in the loyal states. This might have been the case in his state and also in New England, but not elsewhere. The Michigan governor was wrong when he wrote that the address "silence[d] discontent amongst the disloyal elements in the loyal states" after a summer of great dissatisfaction and gloom.[53] Actually, Lincoln's emancipation policy and his suspension of the writ of habeas corpus, which the Republican governors had endorsed, increased political dissent in the lower North and in the border states. The spiraling opposition to these policies, as well as lingering doubts about the war, hurt the Republicans in the fall elections. Although Lincoln's party retained a majority in Congress and won the upper North, it lost the governorship of New York and control of the Indiana and Illinois legislatures.[54]

Lincoln acknowledged the important contribution that the governors had made at Altoona to the Union cause in the war. Governor Blair wrote that "the unanimous agreement of the loyal Governors to sustain the administration" was especially gratifying to the president. Furthermore, Blair said, though without being specific, their work had an "influence upon the future policy of the administration."[55] Governor Curtin also recalled that Lincoln regarded the Altoona conference and the governors' address as "of estimable service to the cause of the Union."[56] The fact that the governors had ignored the Radicals' demand for a reorganization of the cabinet and the military command especially pleased the president.[57] After the war, former Confederate vice president Alexander H. Stephens asserted that the Altoona conference "had delivered the most destructive blow to the South in 1862, when [Southerners] believed that the North was on the point of surrendering the conflict." He "expressed the conviction that but for that conference the North would have been [so] demoralized by the emancipation proclamation and the failures of the Union army that peace would have come on some compromise and honorable basis."[58] Stephens, however, obviously exaggerated the importance of the conference in preventing a compromise peace.

The results of the Altoona conference represented an important success for the governors and Lincoln, working in tandem to save the Union and end slavery. With the notable exception of Democrats Horatio Seymour of New York and Joel Parker of New Jersey, both elected governors in November 1862, the spirit of cooperation between the governors and the president continued until the end of the war.[59] Even though the president and the War Department soon assumed the leading role in raising troops, the Republican or Union Party governors, despite occasional disagreements with the national administration, provided the vital support that Lincoln needed to pursue his war policies.

Regardless of the work of the governors, however, the results of the fall 1862 elections in the North produced a new political crisis for Lincoln and his party, which was soon fueled by the federal military disaster at Fredericksburg in December and the ongoing carnage on the battlefield. In 1863, the state capitals and local communities became the scenes of an intense struggle over the war, civil liberties, and emancipation that threatened to undermine Lincoln and the War Department's ability to suppress the Southern rebellion. Again, the governors were at the center of this struggle.

John A. Andrew, Republican governor of Massachusetts, 1861–66. *John Albion Andrew*, photograph by unknown photographer, no date; from Portraits of American Abolitionists, photograph number 81.12, Massachusetts Historical Society; courtesy of the Massachusetts Historical Society, Boston.

John Brough, Union Party (Republican) governor of Ohio, 1864–65. Courtesy of the Ohio Historical Society, Columbus, Ohio.

Andrew G. Curtin, Republican governor of Pennsylvania, 1861–67. Courtesy of the Library Company of Philadelphia, Philadelphia, Pennsylvania.

Samuel J. Kirkwood, Republican governor of Iowa, 1860–64. Courtesy of the Library of Congress, Washington, D.C.

Oliver P. Morton, Republican governor of Indiana, 1861–67. Courtesy of the Library of Congress, Washington, D.C.

Alexander Ramsey, Republican governor of Minnesota, 1860–63. Courtesy of the Library of Congress, Washington, D.C.

Horatio Seymour, Democratic governor of New York, 1863–64. Courtesy of the Library of Congress, Washington, D.C.

David Tod, Union Party (Republican) governor of Ohio, 1862–64. Courtesy of the Ohio Historical Society, Columbus, Ohio.

Richard Yates, Republican governor of Illinois, 1861–65. Courtesy of the Library of Congress, Washington, D.C.

GOVERNOR SEYMOUR AND
THE COPPERHEAD THREAT

The Democratic Party, which had been splintered earlier by the Republican-led Union coalition, reemerged phoenix-like in 1862 to rally Northern dissidents and party faithful in opposition to Lincoln's policies and in many cases to the war itself. The Democrats prepared for the fall state and local elections in a climate of bitter political divisions. A rising peace faction within the party gained considerable support in the West (today's Midwest), and it threatened to undermine the influence of old Democratic supporters of the war like Governor David Tod of Ohio, who had been important in the Union coalition. Nowhere was the political conflict more evident than in the lower North and in New York and New Jersey.

Democratic editors and activists like Congressman Clement Vallandigham, a rising Ohio peace leader, vigorously assailed Lincoln's Emancipation Proclamation and the arrest of political opponents. Lower North Democrats, joined by border state Unionists and some conservative Republicans, predicted that the effect of Lincoln's proclamation would be an invasion of their states by freed blacks from the South, who would inevitably create tremendous social and racial problems for their communities.[1] Farther north in the fall, New York gubernatorial candidate Horatio Seymour, who normally shunned extremism in his political discourse, leveled his campaign guns on Lincoln's preliminary Emancipation Proclamation. It was "a proposal," he excitedly asserted, "for the butchery of women and children, for scenes of lust and rapine, and of arson and murder, which would invoke the interference of civilized Europe." Later, in a more restrained mood, Seymour provided the campaign slogan for the Democrats when he proclaimed, "The Union as it was, and the Constitution as it is."[2] This catchphrase became the Democratic rallying cry for the remainder of the war.

Denunciation of Lincoln's suspension of the writ of habeas corpus on September 24, 1862, became a major staple of Seymour and the Democratic campaign. Democratic spokesmen claimed that suspension of the writ, designed by Lincoln to prevent interference with the militia draft and the recruitment of army volunteers, would inevitably lead to arbitrary arrests and the detention of dissidents by overzealous Republican officials and military officers. Claiming that they were not disloyal, Peace Democrats, or Copperheads, declared that the war could not be won except at the cost of even greater casualties, the continued violation of civil liberties in the Union states, and the further disruption of the republic of the founders.

Republicans answered with an unrelenting campaign against their Democratic opponents, routinely charging them with disloyalty. Union Republican governors and local leaders bombarded Lincoln with reports of "treason" in their states. Governor Morton became especially persistent in claiming conspiracies to seize control of Indiana as well as Ohio and Illinois. These plots, according to Morton, were the work of a secret society known as the Knights of the Golden Circle, an extreme group of antiwar zealots. The startling success of militant Democrats in winning a majority in the Indiana legislature in the October 14 election seemed to confirm Morton's fears. It is not known just how dangerous or disloyal the Knights really were, but probably most Copperheads, though supporting peace and opposing arbitrary arrests and emancipation, did not favor the South.[3]

Morton also continued to remind Lincoln of the secessionist threat to seize Kentucky, which came close to reality in the late summer and fall of 1862, when the rebel armies of Braxton Bragg and Edmund Kirby Smith invaded the Bluegrass State. Although the rebel armies were repulsed at Perryville, Morton anxiously telegraphed the president after the battle. "The butchery of our troops . . . was terrible," he wrote, and he believed this was a prelude to rebel success in Kentucky. The Confederates retreated to Tennessee after the Battle of Perryville. Still, Morton frantically informed Lincoln, "Nothing but success, speedy and decided, will save our cause from utter destruction." "In the Northwest," he reported, "distrust and despair are seizing upon the hearts of the people."[4]

The Indiana governor hurriedly made plans for him and Governor Yates to go to Washington and impress on Lincoln the seriousness of military and political affairs in the West and the need for a change in the conduct of the war. Morton proposed to Yates that the two governors demand the removal of General Don Carlos Buell as commander of the Union forces in the region. Before Morton and Yates had left for Washington, however, Lincoln, disturbed by what he heard from the governors and others, replaced Buell with General William S. Rosecrans. Pleased with the news, Morton and Yates telegraphed the president, "The removal of General Buell could not have been delayed an hour with safety to the army or the cause." The governors told Lincoln, "The action you have taken renders our visit unnecessary, although we are very desirous to confer with you in regard to the general condition of the Northwest."[5]

Instead of going to Washington, Morton wrote a long letter to the president on October 27, describing the grave situation in the West. He informed Lincoln that the strong likelihood of Democratic success throughout the lower North in the elections was leading "the Democratic politicians of Ohio, Indiana and Illinois [to] assume that the rebellion will not be crushed, and that the independence of the rebel Confederacy will, before many months, be practically acknowledged." What, then, Morton asked, "shall be the destiny" of these three states? The governor answered his own question. The Democrats of Ohio, Indiana, and Illinois (he could have added Kentucky and Missouri) would take their states out of the Union and form a new government—"a Northwestern Confederacy—as a preparatory step to annexation with the South." He told the president that this "programme" had been "the staple of every Democratic speech." As before, Morton exaggerated the western Democratic desire to become part of the Southern Confederacy. The Democrats, he said, repeatedly declare that the people of the West "had no interests or sympathies in common with the people of the Northern and Eastern states; that New England is fattening at our expense; that the people of New England are cold, selfish, money-making, and, through the medium of tariffs and railroads, are pressing us to the dust."[6]

Morton told Lincoln that the Democrats (in this letter, he did not use the pejorative term "traitors" for the opposition) insist "that socially and commercially their sympathies and interests are with the people of the Southern states." He maintained that they could "never consent to be separated politically from the people who control" the Mississippi River, "the great artery and outlet of all Western commerce." This war, the Democrats contended and Morton reported, had "been forced upon the South for the purpose of abolishing slavery." The governor admitted that "some of these arguments [contained] much truth," including the West's "geographical and social relations" with the South. "But the most potent appeal is that connected with the free navigation and control of the Mississippi river."[7]

Revealing his own deep concern, as well as that of other western Republicans, the Indiana governor predicted a calamitous scenario for the war and the Union if the situation did not improve: "Should the misfortune of our arms, or other causes, compel us to the abandonment of this war and the concession of the independence of the rebel states—Ohio, Indiana and Illinois can only be prevented from a new act of secession by a bloody and desolating civil war." The efforts of western Republicans "must then be directed to the preservation of what is left; to maintaining in the union those [states] which are truly loyal, and to retaining the territories of the West."[8]

Although the West was more ethnically, culturally, and economically diverse than New England, Morton's characterization of western animosity toward the "Yankees" of the Northeast was overblown. After all, the people of both sections had similar political and legal institutions and in most cases devoutly wanted the Union to be preserved. Furthermore, many in the West, particularly in the upper regions, were from New England or upstate New York and, along with recent arrivals from Germany, backed the war and the

Republican Party. They also opposed slavery, though they did not necessarily favor federal emancipation at this time.

The movement for a Northwest confederacy, or an alliance with the South, was supported by a large number of Democrats in the lower West. However, the chances of these states leaving the Union, though frightening to Morton and the Republicans, was only speculative. Indeed, the real objective of most western Democrats was to end the horrific war in the South and restore respect for constitutional rights at home, as they interpreted these rights. Their suspicion of Republican intentions extended back to the prewar political contests and the belief, cultivated by Democratic leaders and the press, that the antislavery movement was the cause of secession and the war. They had become convinced that their lives and liberties were at stake in the hands of Lincoln, the Republican Congress, and local Republicans. Western Democrats in 1862 unrealistically believed that the success of the peace movement would lead to the restoration of the Union, the reopening of the Mississippi River and Southern railroads, and the revival of markets for western commerce.

As a solution to the western problem, Governor Morton backed a military plan, initially proposed by General John A. McClernand of Illinois, to free the Mississippi River for commerce, defeat the rebels in the lower South, and save the West for the Union. McClernand had also gained the support of Governor Yates for his plan, which called for an independent expedition to open the river for the Union. McClernand expected to command the military force. Yates, recognizing the political importance of such a campaign and also McClernand's status as a military hero among western Democrats, on September 20 directed the general to go to Washington and lobby the president and cabinet members for his plan.[9]

On October 20, Lincoln, following the Democratic victory in the Indiana elections and after talking to McClernand, approved a "confidential" order for the Mississippi River campaign. The order, sent by Secretary of War Stanton, directed the Illinois general "to proceed to the States of Indiana, Illinois and Iowa, to organize the troops remaining in those States" for "a sufficient force, not required by the operations of General Grant's command," to operate "against Vicksburg and to clear the Mississippi river and open navigation to New Orleans." Although marked "confidential" for the time being, the president informed Stanton that the order could be shown to the governors. He added, "I feel deep interest in the success of the expedition, and desire it to be pushed forward with all possible dispatch." Lincoln expected the recruitment of the troops for the campaign to be done through the auspices of the governors.[10]

After meeting with McClernand on October 22, Governor Morton outlined to Lincoln what the expedition could achieve: "All obstacles to the navigation of the Mississippi river" would be removed by the campaign, accompanied by "the thorough conquest of the states upon its western bank." "The river," he asserted, "once in our possession and occupied by our gunboats can never be crossed by a rebel army, and the fighting men" of Arkansas, Louisiana, and Texas "can never get back to [the] relief of their states." Morton, who for political reasons in Indiana had not previously demonstrated any enthusiasm for emancipation, now argued that in order to make the conquest of the lower Mississippi valley "thorough and complete," Lincoln's Emancipation Proclamation "should be executed in every county and every township and upon every plantation." "Complete emancipation . . . would place the possession of those states on a very different footing from that of any other rebel territory which we have heretofore overrun." Morton predicted that the conquest of the lower Mississippi could "be done in less than ninety days with an army of less than one hundred thousand men." "The accomplishment of this plan," the governor claimed, "will [guarantee] the loyalty of the Northwestern states by the assurance that whatever may be the result of the war, the free navigation and control of the Mississippi river will be secured at all events."[11] Lincoln probably had not yet received Morton's disturbing letter of October 27 on the crisis in the West when, on October 30, Stanton issued the final orders, no longer a secret, for the campaign to proceed under McClernand's command.[12]

The Indiana, Illinois, and Iowa governors acted immediately to aid McClernand in obtaining recruits for the Mississippi expedition. Along with the support of the governors, McClernand could report to Lincoln on December 12 that he had raised forty thousand troops for the campaign.[13] Still, he anticipated resistance in the War Department to his independent army, though technically it would be under General Grant's overall command in the region. Earlier, on November 10, McClernand had warned Lincoln, whom he had known before the war, that if such opposition developed, "or for other causes, the expedition [became] an uncertainty," the political consequences in the West would be disastrous.[14]

Opposition to the Mississippi expedition and the hopes of the western governors, as McClernand expected, soon came from the military high command. On the same day that McClernand warned Lincoln about possible obstacles to his campaign, General Grant at LaGrange, Tennessee, telegraphed General in Chief Henry W. Halleck, "Am I to understand that you want me to lie still here while an expedition is fitted out from Memphis, or do you want me to push as far south as possible [toward Vicksburg]?" Halleck disliked political generals, particularly those who, like McClernand, wrote directly to Lincoln and Stanton. He replied to Grant, "You have command of all [troops] sent to your department, [and] have permission to fight the enemy where you please." Although Grant initially provided a modicum of support for the Mississippi expedition, he also believed that McClernand was "unmanageable and incompetent."[15]

Halleck permitted Grant to reduce McClernand's force and ordered the Illinois general to join Grant's main army. "It was the wish of the President," Halleck wrote Grant, that "McClernand's corps shall constitute a part of the river expedition and that he shall have the immediate command under your direction." Realizing that he would be a subordinate of Grant's, the Illinois political general was furious and blamed Halleck for the loss of his independent command. McClernand wrote to Lincoln, charging the general in chief "with willful contempt of superior authority" by violating the secretary of war's order giving him "the command of the proposed 'Miss. River Expedition.'" He demanded that the president dismiss Halleck and "take upon [himself] the exercise of his functions" as general in chief. By removing Halleck, McClernand cheekily told Lincoln, "you will remove an anomaly in the organization of our armies—an anomaly incompatible with its unity and responsibility." The president merely marked the envelope containing the letter with McClernand's name and date. Wisely, he did not intervene in the matter.[16]

McClernand refused to give up easily. After taking Arkansas Post on the Arkansas River before joining Grant's army in the siege of Vicksburg, he appealed to Governor Yates for support. On February 16, he wrote to the governor, "A revolution is impending in the Northwest. I need not remind you that with the actual inception of this revolution" in 1862, "the cause of the union [has been] seriously endangered, if not lost." McClernand, with his own command in mind, urged Yates to demand that the president hasten the suppression of all rebel resistance west of the Mississippi River as a vital part of the strategy "to crush" the revolution. He told the Illinois governor, "I would have wrested Arkansas and Louisiana by this time from the rebellion but for a blind order restraining me. With the west bank reclaimed, the destiny of the Northwest will not be blighted, [and] our arms will ultimately triumph over all resistance to the National Authority."[17]

Although Yates agreed with McClernand, he refused to intercede with Lincoln in the controversy; after all, an Illinois general, U. S. Grant, was in control of the campaign to clear the Mississippi Valley of rebels. Nonetheless, Yates protested to Lincoln after Grant's dismissal of McClernand from command on June 18, 1863, for continued insubordination. Joined by Lincoln's Illinois friends Ozias M. Hatch and Jesse K. Dubois, the governor informed the president of "a deep and general . . . dissatisfaction at the dismissal of Gen'l McClernand from his late Command." Yates, Hatch, and Dubois reminded Lincoln that McClernand's "name [was] indissolubly blended with most, if not all the great military actions and events occurring in the South West." Furthermore, he was a pillar of political strength to the Union cause in the West. They told Lincoln that the general's recent speeches in Illinois, "exhorting the people to persevere until the rebellion was crushed," had had a timely effect in boosting morale and reversing the dismal political situation for the Union Party in the state.[18]

Lincoln was well aware of McClernand's political strength in Illinois, especially in the southern part of the state, where Copperheads were creating severe problems for army recruitment and the Union cause. Despite repeated appeals by McClernand, including a forty-page printed statement, Lincoln declined to reinstate him in command. After the president refused to honor the general's request for a court of inquiry, McClernand submitted his letter of resignation, which Lincoln also rejected. But when McClernand resubmitted his resignation after the critical November 1864 elections, Secretary of War Stanton, with Grant's hearty endorsement, approved it.[19] Lincoln must have been glad finally to be rid of this troublesome political general. This time, no western governor came to McClernand's defense.

Throughout the lower North and in New York and New Jersey, the Democrats, spearheaded by an aroused Copperhead minority, made substantial gains in the fall 1862 elections. The Democratic surge created deep concern for Lincoln and holdover Republican governors in the free states. Even in relatively safe Republican states, governors like Kirkwood of Iowa, Salomon of Wisconsin, and Buckingham of Connecticut had to beat back Democratic challenges, which they routinely associated with the Copperheads and treason. In the case of Connecticut, where the elections did not occur until April 1863, Buckingham won reelection by only three thousand votes.[20] Fortunately for the Republicans and the prosecution of the war, no gubernatorial elections occurred in the lower western states, Pennsylvania, or the border states, with the exception of Delaware, where a staunch Unionist won. In the lower North, repeated Republican charges of Democratic disloyalty did not negate voter opposition to Lincoln's emancipation policy, his suspension of the writ of habeas corpus, the arrest of dissidents by zealous Union officials and army officers, and the seemingly unending battlefield carnage. Most Democrats still openly supported the war to preserve the Union, but the election demonstrated that antiwar sentiment was growing in the party and in the closely contested states.

In addition to the Indiana legislature, Democrats gained control of the Illinois General Assembly, winning the congressional state-at-large seat and eight of the other thirteen seats. Also troubling to the president and to Governor Yates was that the legislature would inevitably replace Lincoln's friend, Orville H. Browning, in the U.S. Senate with a Democrat. Yates blamed Lincoln for the Republican debacle in Illinois, particularly his failure to adopt more vigorous policies for winning the war and to appoint competent commanders.[21] Probably more important in the Republican defeat in Lincoln's home state were his unwise decisions, virtually on the eve of the fall elections, to issue the preliminary Emancipation Proclamation and suspend the writ of habeas corpus.

In Ohio, Democrats carried their state ticket by a majority of 5,577 votes and captured fourteen of the nineteen seats in Congress.[22] (The Ohio governorship was not at stake in the election.) In Pennsylvania, the Democrats claimed a victory, yet they failed to gain control of both houses of the legislature. However, their representation in the U.S. House of Representatives increased from seven to eleven members.[23] In traditionally Democratic New Jersey, Joel Parker won a relatively easy victory over the Republican candidate for governor. Parker, a Douglas Democrat in 1860, proved to be a dynamic governor who, while supporting the war, argued that Lincoln's policies would fail to suppress the rebellion. The Emancipation Proclamation, Parker contended, would cause the rebels to fight harder. The Democrats increased their majority in the New Jersey legislature and captured four of the state's five seats in the U.S. House of Representatives.[24] Nationally, the Democrats gained thirty-four members in the House of Representatives but fell short of a majority even with the support of border state conservatives.

The most startling Democratic victory in the fall 1862 elections occurred in New York. There, former governor Horatio Seymour, running on a platform of "The Union as it was, and the Constitution as it is," which included opposition to the Emancipation Proclamation, defeated General James S. Wadsworth, commander of the Washington Military District and a stalwart antislavery Republican. The Democrats, however, failed by a small margin to gain control of the New York legislature.

The New England states remained true to the Republican Party. Still, Governor Andrew of Massachusetts saw Copperhead "traitors" behind every woodpile and feared that the elections elsewhere would seriously weaken the war effort. He had cause for some concern. In Massachusetts, fifty thousand voters opposed Andrew's reelection; he received seventy thousand votes.[25] The states of the relatively sparsely populated West, now including Kansas, continued to vote Republican, though in Wisconsin only Governor Salomon's success in securing legislation to permit the soldiers to vote in the field saved the state for the "Union Republicans."[26] In the Far West, Republicans earlier had replaced Democrats as governors of California and Oregon. These states, though also experiencing a Copperhead surge, remained true to Lincoln and the Union, due in no small part to the efforts of Governors Leland Stanford in California and Addison Gibbs in Oregon.[27]

In early 1863, the Democrats in New York, New Jersey, Indiana, and Illinois moved quickly to take charge of their states and reverse Republican war policies, including Lincoln's Emancipation Proclamation. Seymour, in his inaugural address of January 7, sounded the clarion call for Democratic resistance to what he characterized as the unconstitutional acts of the Republicans in the states as well as in Washington. Devoting more than two-thirds of his speech to national affairs, the New York governor clearly reached for the leadership of the anti-Radical movement in the North while expressing Democratic support for the war to preserve the Union. He decried the extremism of both New England and the South. To save the Union and end the terrible war, Seymour called for a coalition of "the central and western states," which, he said, held the balance of power between the Radicals of New England and the secessionists of the South. Seymour maintained that if the Union were ever to be restored "as it was," sectional interests and radicalism must be denied a voice in the federal government. He insisted that the masses of Northern voters supported neither secession nor abolition. Until changes could occur, he said, "we must accept the condition of affairs as they stand. At this moment the fortunes of our country are influenced by the results of the battles. Our armies in the field must be supported; all constitutional demands of our General Government must be promptly responded to."[28] As would soon become apparent, the question was what constituted legitimate "constitutional demands" for the New York governor.

Governor Parker of New Jersey, in his inaugural address on January 20, 1863, also lashed out against Lincoln's policies. He denounced the president's curtailment of civil liberties and predicted a slave revolt and a massacre of blacks if the Emancipation Proclamation was enforced. Driven further by the bloody repulse of Union forces at Fredericksburg in December 1862, the New Jersey legislature adopted Copperhead resolutions calling for an end to the war.[29] Despite his sharp criticism of what he referred to as Lincoln's "unconstitutional" policies, Parker, reflecting the will of the majority in his state, continued to support the war.

In the West, Governor David Tod of Ohio, shaken by the fall election returns in his state, began to appoint old Democratic associates to office, but not Copperheads. Although he had supported emancipation at the Altoona conference, Tod, in his annual message to the Ohio legislature two days after Lincoln signed the Emancipation Proclamation, made no mention of the decree of freedom. The governor issued a mea culpa for having acquiesced in the suspension of the writ of habeas corpus and for military arrests in the state. However, he asked the legislature to increase its support for the troops, a more efficient militia to defend the state, and the right of Ohio soldiers to vote in the field. Secretary of War Stanton, in need of encouraging news from the major western states and probably expressing Lincoln's sentiments also, telegraphed Tod, "I have just read with great pleasure your manly and patriotic message. You deserve not only the honor and respect of your great State, but also of every loyal and patriotic heart." Tod had earlier opposed the recruitment of black troops, which had been authorized by the Emancipation Proclamation, but in May he asked the War Department for approval to raise an African American regiment in the state.[30]

Next door in Indiana, Governor Morton, to no one's surprise after the fall election, became entangled in a bitter struggle over the war with the newly elected Democratic legislature. The air in Indianapolis was thick with wild rumors of conspiracies when the General Assembly met in early January 1863. The excitable governor reported to Secretary of War Stanton on January 3 that the Democrats intended "to pass a resolution acknowledging the Southern Confederacy, and urging the States of the Northwest to dissolve all constitutional relations with the New England States." "The same thing is on foot in Illinois," he claimed.[31] The majority of Democrats in neither state legislature, however, had any such dark purposes in mind. They responded to Morton's charge that they plotted revolution by insisting that, though opposed to the Republicans, they were not disloyal and only wanted peace on the basis of reunion and the restoration of constitutional rights. Still, resolutions by the Democrats in the Indiana legislature praising Governor Seymour of New York for his "exalted and patriotic sentiments" in his inaugural address and acknowledging him as their leader did nothing to lessen the governor's concern regarding a Copperhead conspiracy.

On January 31, the Indiana governor urgently telegraphed Lincoln, requesting that the president meet him in Harrisburg, Pennsylvania, for a conference on the crisis and an appeal for federal help against the Copperheads. Lincoln refused, explaining that such a meeting "would be misconstrued a thousand ways." "Of course," he admitted, "if the whole truth could be told and accepted as the truth," it would be different; "but that is impossible."[32] Perhaps remembering Morton's earlier exaggerated reports on the political situation in the Ohio Valley, Lincoln probably concluded that it would be wise to await events before considering a politically risky intervention in the Hoosier State.

Having failed to secure the meeting with the president, Morton again, as he had done in the fall, wrote a long letter to Lincoln describing the dire "condition of affairs in Indiana and the North West generally." He sent the prominent social reformer Robert Dale Owen to deliver the letter to the president and explain in detail the need for Lincoln's "immediate consideration" of affairs in the West. "The Democratic scheme," Morton wrote to Lincoln, was to "end the war by any means whatever at the earliest moment," which meant recognizing the Southern Confederacy. The Democrats "will then propose to the Rebels a re-union and re-construction upon the condition of leaving out the New England States; this they believe the Rebel leaders will accept and so do I." The Indiana governor claimed that "Govr. Seymour and the leading Democratic politicians of New York and Pennsylvania [were] in the scheme and hope to be able to carry their States for it." Even if New York and Pennsylvania would "not embark in this scheme," western Democrats, Morton insisted, had "determined to go on without them."[33]

Governor Morton claimed that "every democratic paper" and speech in Indiana was "teeming with abuse of New England and it is the theme of every speech." The Democrats, the governor told the president, charged that New England, in addition to its iniquitous economic actions, "has brought upon us, the war by a fanatical crusade against Slavery." These views, he reported to Lincoln, "[are] already entertained by the mass of the Democratic party, and there is great danger of their spreading until they are embraced by a large majority of our people." Secret societies like the Knights of the Golden Circle, Morton asserted, "are being established in every County and Township in the State of Indiana" to promote the Democratic peace agenda. Immediate action by the federal government, he insisted, should be taken to counteract the Copperheads in the West, including a more vigorous prosecution of the war against the South.[34]

A petty quarrel between the General Assembly and Morton over the submission of his annual message and angry memorials from pro-Republican troops in the field heightened the tension in Indiana in early 1863 and prompted the governor to order the arrests of numerous suspected "traitors" throughout the state.[35] Incensed by Morton's actions, the Democrats debated legislation to limit the powers of the governor. An impasse soon occurred between the two branches of the Hoosier State government when the Democrats introduced a bill designed to give their party control of the state military board. On February 25–26, all but four of the Republican members of the House of Representatives, with the governor's support, bolted the House to prevent a quorum and thus the passage of the military bill. They went to Madison, Indiana, on the Ohio River, preparatory to fleeing to Kentucky to avoid a forced recall by the Democrats. Instead of compromising with the Republicans on the military bill, the General Assembly adjourned on March 8 without passing a two-year appropriations bill and other measures. Morton, claiming that it would be a waste of time for the legislature to meet, refused to call a special session to pass a budget. The legislature did not convene again until early 1865, after the Republicans had regained control. For two years, beginning in 1863, Morton railed against the Copperheads in the legislature, as well as Democrats generally.[36]

Until the legislature reconvened, Governor Morton had a practical problem: how to finance the expanded Indiana government and meet the military needs without state appropriations. Morton appealed to the War Department for financial support. Possibly with Lincoln's approval, he obtained $250,000 in U.S. Treasury warrants from a special fund that Secretary of War Stanton had established. The resourceful and aggressive governor, in order to keep the state government running, also received money through extralegal means, from Republican counties and private donors.[37] Morton used the funds to wage a campaign of suppression against the Democrats and Copperheads, whom he routinely referred to as "traitors." The governor became a hero to the impatient Radical Republicans in the North, in contrast to Lincoln, whom they characterized as weak and unable to take effective action against the Copperheads and the Southern rebels.

The political situation in Illinois in early 1863 was hardly more promising than in Indiana for the Republicans and ardent supporters of the war. There, Governor Yates also faced the hostile Democratic legislature that had been elected in 1862, but he handled the situation with more skill than Morton. The Republican minority in the General Assembly, instead of bolting the regular session, as occurred in Indiana, launched a filibuster when the Democratic legislators offered resolutions demanding a cease-fire in the war followed by a national convention in Louisville, Kentucky, to restore the Union. Both Yates and Lincoln realized that adoption of the resolutions, if they gained national support, would mean Confederate independence. The filibuster ended when the Democratic and Republican members reached an agreement to postpone consideration of the resolutions and deal with the regular business of the General Assembly.

After approval of the appropriations and legislative apportionment bills, which were signed by Yates, the Illinois legislature adjourned until June. By that time, the Democrats believed, they would have gained sufficient public support to ensure the passage of their resolutions. When the General Assembly reconvened in June, the Democrats again raised the banner of peace and also introduced a habeas corpus bill designed to prevent illegal arrests in the state. Governor Yates had had enough of Copperhead opposition to the war. He prorogued the legislature, which took the Democrats by surprise, as an Illinois governor had never before taken such a drastic action. With the already appropriated money, Yates was able to maintain the state government and aid the war effort. As in Indiana, the Illinois General Assembly did not meet again until after the Republicans had regained a majority in the 1864 elections.[38]

Governor Yates's prorogue of the legislature, the Emancipation Proclamation, and the federal attempt to enforce conscription spurred a wave of violence in Illinois during the spring and summer of 1863. A virtual civil war threatened to break out in Illinois. With the West in mind, Lincoln told Senator Charles Sumner that he feared "a fire in the rear" more than he did the rebel armies.[39] Federal and state Republican officials in Illinois, as in Indiana, began to round up and incarcerate "traitors." Between June 1 and October 10, more than two thousand arrests were made in Lincoln's home state alone. Even some prominent Illinois Republicans like Senator Lyman Trumbull protested the arrests and Lincoln's suspension of the writ of habeas corpus, but with limited success.[40]

In nearby Iowa, Governor Samuel Kirkwood feared an outbreak of rebellion and civil war in the state if the War Department did not supply him with the necessary arms for his militia or home guard. "A secret organization, known popularly as the Knights of the Golden Circle," he wrote Stanton on March 13, "is widely spread through the State, the object of which, as I am informed and believe, is to embarrass the Government in the prosecution of the war, mainly by encouraging desertions from the Army, protecting deserters from arrest, discouraging enlistments, [and] preparing the public mind for armed resistance to a [federal] conscription" of Iowans. As elsewhere in the region, the Copperhead plan in Iowa, Kirkwood told Stanton—and thus Lincoln—was to unite the Northwest with the Confederate States.[41]

Although the governor exaggerated the threat of rebellion in the state, violent clashes between Unionists and armed antiwar zealots occurred, particularly in the southern tier of counties bordering on Missouri. Kirkwood dispatched home guard units to the threatened counties, where, with arms evidently provided by the War Department, they restored order. At one antiwar camp, home guard companies dispersed one thousand Copperheads in what became known as the "Skunk River War." Resistance to Union authorities was further reduced by the ability of the state to meet its conscription quota with volunteers.[42]

General Ambrose E. Burnside, however, made matters worse in the lower western states when, on April 13, 1863, as commander of the Department of Ohio, he issued General Order Number 38, providing for the military arrest of rebel sympathizers. The order implied that criticism of the war in any form was treason.[43] Burnside's imprisonment of Clement L. Vallandigham, the region's most notorious Copperhead, and the suspension of the Democratic *Chicago Times*, an order that Lincoln promptly and wisely revoked, created further unrest in the lower West and in Kentucky and Missouri.

Morton and the border state governors realized that Burnside's actions played into the hands of the Copperheads, further damaging support for the war in their states and making life more difficult for them. The Indiana governor reversed his earlier effort to secure Lincoln's intervention against the Copperheads when, on May 30, he asked the president to rescind Burnside's martial law order. Morton explained that it "supersede[d] civil authority in Ohio, Indiana and Illinois," where, he claimed, "the Administration of the laws continued unimpaired." The effect of the order, Morton informed Lincoln, was "bad," and it was "greatly intensifying the hatred of the masses of the Democratic party, toward the Government." Burnside's action, the governor reported, was "rapidly converting what in many, was mere clamor and general opposition to the Administration into bitter hostility to the Government and the War." Even though the order "was not issued with your knowledge, or by your authority, yet your subsequent silence gives it your ratification before the public." Morton advised the president that, as a matter of prudent policy, "the preservation of the peace and loyalty of the North Western States had better be left with the State authorities, to be aided and supported by Federal power when necessary."[44]

Other Republicans as well as Democrats had informed the president of the damaging political effect of Burnside's order and the general's arrest of Vallandigham. On May 20, Lincoln, Stanton, and General in Chief Henry W. Halleck conferred on the troublesome issue. None wanted to repudiate fully what Burnside had done. After the meeting, Halleck wrote to Burnside, "No objections were made to your actions in this matter but there was evidently some embarrassment in regard to the disposition of the prisoner [Vallandigham]. Outside friends have expressed fears that this case might do more harm than good." Halleck, speaking for the president, cautioned Burnside to interfere with civil tribunals "as little as possible" in loyal states like Ohio. "Treasonable acts in those States unless of immediate and pressing danger should be left for trial by the courts."[45]

In response to the rebuke, Burnside offered to be relieved of his command. Lincoln, upset that the general had put him and support for the war in such a difficult position, shot back, "When I shall wish to supersede you I will let you know. All the cabinet regretted the necessity of arresting [Vallandigham], some perhaps, doubting, that there was a real necessity for it—but, being done, all were for seeing you through with it."[46] Lincoln commuted Vallandigham's prison sentence to exile in the Confederacy. Although Burnside's repressive order died a silent death, the president left intact federal and state acts suspending the writ of habeas corpus and imprisoning dissidents without trials.

Meanwhile, the passage of the first federal conscription act in American history kept the cauldron of dissent boiling in the West and elsewhere. Enacted on March 3, 1863, the Enrollment (Conscription) Act gave the War Department, not the states, in contrast to the Militia Act of 1862, the authority to prepare for the drafting of able-bodied young men who were not in the army. The War Department, to the dismay of some governors who perceived their authority diminished, appointed provost marshals for each state who would report directly to the provost marshal general in Washington. A clause in the Enrollment Act permitted an eligible person to avoid the draft by paying $300 to the government. This commutation exemption suggested to many people the proverbial judgment of "a rich man's war, but a poor man's fight." The exemption immediately created a wave of protest, even in areas where support for the war was strong.[47]

Governor Morton, though favoring military conscription as a necessity, immediately wrote to the president that the commutation provision would further erode support for the war in Indiana and elsewhere. Three days after the passage of the Enrollment Act, Morton appealed to Lincoln to prohibit the execution of this provision in the act. He reported to the president, "I can assure you that this feature in the Bill is creating much excitement and ill feeling towards the Government among the poorer classes generally, without regard to party," in the West. If not checked by the removal of the commutation clause, it could "lead to a popular storm under cover of which the execution of the Conscription Act may be greatly hindered or even defeated in some portions of the Country." Already, Morton told Lincoln, "movements are on foot in the secret societies of Indiana and among leaders of the disloyalists to raise money to purchase the exemption of every Democrat who may be drafted and who cannot raise the money himself; and already the boast is made that the Government shall not have one more of their men for the prosecution of this War."[48]

As was the practice of several governors when dealing with important state concerns, Morton dispatched agents to visit the president to "more fully inform [him] of the views and apprehensions entertained here" about the commutation provision.[49] Lincoln, however, did not believe that he had the authority to override it, even if he had wanted to; therefore, he refused to intervene. The first draft, following completion of the enrollment of eligible males, occurred in July 1863. One year later, on June 8, 1864, the president secured Congress's repeal of the controversial $300 commutation clause, but not the draft.[50]

Two months before the passage of the Enrollment Act in March 1863, Lincoln had authorized the recruitment of black troops in the Emancipation Proclamation. The border states vehemently opposed the decision, and fears emerged that Kentucky might yet attempt to leave the Union. Lincoln reduced the secession threat by temporarily suspending black enrollment in the Bluegrass State. But when it was restored by Congress in early 1864 with Lincoln's approval, Governor Thomas E. Bramlette, angered by the action, rushed to Washington and reached a tentative agreement with Lincoln that no blacks would be enrolled for military service in counties that met their quotas with white volunteers. Furthermore, troops serving in the Confederate army would not count in determining Kentucky's quota, which reduced the number of white men subject to conscription.[51] Although lower Northern governors at first worried about the political effect of black recruitment, they soon warmed to the idea, especially when the War Department permitted them to fill their draft quotas with African Americans, many to be recruited in the slave states.[52]

Governor Andrew of Massachusetts, even before the president's approval of black troops in the army, vigorously sought the enrollment of African Americans in his state's regiments. No governor became more zealous in applying Lincoln's policy of black recruitment than Andrew. Governor Kirkwood of Iowa explained why he, as well as other governors, many of their constituents, and their soldiers in the field, eventually came to support black enlistments in the army. If black people, Kirkwood declared, were "willing to pay for their freedom by fighting for those who make them free, I am entirely willing that they should do so." He could not "understand or appreciate any policy that insists that all the lives lost and all the constitutions broken down to preserve the country shall be those of white men when black men are to be found willing to do the work and take the risks" of serving in the army.[53]

Beginning in 1863, after they assumed office, the two Democratic governors in the North, Horatio Seymour of New York and Joel Parker of New Jersey, refused to acquiesce quietly to Lincoln's policies. Seymour, governor of the most populous state in the Union, became the leading opponent of conscription, the Emancipation Proclamation, and the suspension of the writ of habeas corpus, all of which he viewed as unconstitutional. However, he always denied the repeated Republican charge that he was disloyal or sought to undermine the war effort. Seymour insisted that the war could not be won at the expense of the constitutional rights of the states and the people. According to the governor, Lincoln's policies, especially emancipation and his unwillingness to negotiate with the South for the restoration of the Union, ensured that the war would be a long, unrelenting conflict. Furthermore, Seymour maintained, the divisions over the war in the loyal states would continue and would culminate in the triumph of those seeking peace without reunion.

In March 1863, Seymour entertained an important visitor from Ohio. This was Clement Vallandigham, who, two months before his arrest by Burnside, was touring the Northeast promoting peace. A cessation of hostilities, he argued, would produce a reconciliation and reunion of the warring sections. Meeting at Albany soon after the passage of the Enrollment Act, the New York governor and the western Copperhead were joined by several prominent Democrats, including former governor William Bigler of Pennsylvania, who had joined the antiwar ranks in the party. All agreed that eastern and western Democrats should unite in opposition to the unconstitutional and radical measures of Lincoln and the Republican-dominated Congress. Seymour, however, questioned Vallandigham's and the Copperheads' peace position. He contended that the Democratic Party, particularly in the Northeast, could not hope for success on an antiwar platform. After several days of discussions, Seymour secured Vallandigham's pledge to tone down his opposition to the war and instead focus his attention on resisting Lincoln's policies through constitutional means and the ballot box.[54]

At the White House, Lincoln read only a partisan and inaccurate account in the Republican *New York Times* of Vallandigham's northeastern tour. This newspaper reported that the Ohio Copperhead in his speeches "opposed the war, advocated immediate peace, [and] denounced our Conscription Act as ten times worse than that of Poland."[55] Lincoln feared that Vallandigham might have persuaded

Seymour, and in turn other eastern Democrats like Governor Parker of New Jersey, to resist the war effort. On March 23, the president wrote Seymour a letter designed to appeal to the governor's patriotism and encourage his support for the administration's policies. Even though "[we] are substantially strangers," Lincoln began, "I write this chiefly that we may become better acquainted. I, for the time being, am at the head of a nation which is in great peril; and you are at the head of the greatest State of that nation. As to maintaining the nation's life, and integrity, I assume, and believe, there can not be a difference of *purpose* between you and me."[56]

The president went on, "If we should differ as to means, it is important that such difference should be as small as possible—that it should not be enhanced by unjust suspicions on one side or the other." Lincoln wanted Seymour to know that he highly valued the importance of the Empire State in the war. "In the performance of my duty," the president told the governor, "the co-operation of your State, as that of others, is needed—in fact, is indispensable. This alone is a sufficient reason why I should wish to be at a good understanding with you." He asked Seymour to write him a letter in response, "saying in it, just what you think fit."[57]

Years later, Thurlow Weed, the influential editor of the *Albany Evening News*, said that Lincoln had authorized him to promise Seymour that Lincoln would make way for the New York governor as his successor as president if the governor supported his war policies. Weed's recollection probably overstated the president's attempt to secure the governor's cooperation.[58] It is highly unlikely that Lincoln would have undermined his own credibility in the Republican Party by agreeing to support Seymour for president in 1864 or 1868 if the governor cooperated with him. Even as a gesture of goodwill toward Seymour, which Republicans and others would have misunderstood, the president could hardly have made such a risky proposal.

Seymour finally replied briefly on April 14 to the president's March 23 letter. He told Lincoln that he had been too busy with "official duties" to prepare a long paper that would "state clearly the aspect of public affairs from [his] stand point." However, he assured the president that the views held by him were "entertained by one half of the population of the Northern States." "No political resentments, or no personal objects will turn me aside from the pathway I have marked out for myself," Seymour asserted. He promised to demonstrate "to those charged with the Administration of public affairs a due deference and respect and to yield them a just and generous support in all measures they may adopt within the scope of their Constitutional powers [for] the preservation of the Union."[59]

Governor Seymour soon demonstrated that he had no intention of cooperating with Lincoln on vital issues regarding habeas corpus, military arrests, emancipation, and federal military conscription. As the first draft following the enrollment of men approached, Seymour turned his rhetorical guns on the Lincoln administration, particularly its conscription policy. In a speech in Brooklyn on the Fourth of July, one day after the climactic three-day battle at Gettysburg, the governor reportedly exclaimed that neither Congress nor the president, without the consent of state authorities, had the right to force a man "to take part in the ungodly conflict which is distracting the land." Seymour was careful to mention that he had sent the state militia to defend the Northeast against General Lee's forces. In his Brooklyn address, he attacked Lincoln's doctrine of necessity as a justification for his violations of the Constitution, including the suppression of the press and individual liberties. The Democratic governor reminded his audience of the American revolutionary tradition that "liberty was born in war; it does not die in [civil] war." He wanted the courts to rule on the constitutionality of conscription before the first draft occurred. Seymour declared that the administration in Washington was "hostile to [the] rights and liberties" of the people," and he suggested that the Lincoln government should be obeyed only as long as it did not transgress on its constitutional powers. The New York governor admonished the people to hold the federal government's feet to the fire concerning the protection of state and individual rights.[60]

On July 11, the first draft in New York under federal military conscription occurred with little outward hostility, despite Seymour's fiery Fourth of July speech in Brooklyn. But wild rumors quickly spread, and violent incidents in the streets of New York City spawned mob action, which soon degenerated into the worst riot in American history. It also was fueled by the unleashing of white working-class and immigrant hostility toward black people and middle-class Republicans. Governor Seymour, who was at Long Branch, New Jersey, when the rioting began on Monday, July 13, was unable to return to the city until the next day. When he arrived, he found areas of the city engulfed in violence, including the destruction of property, looting, and arson. Only an overwhelmed police force and small units of troops, including marines from the harbor, stood against the rioters.

The governor immediately went to City Hall, where on the steps he delivered an impromptu address, the report of which was distorted by the city's Republican press and effectively used against him. He allegedly addressed the "mob" as "my friends" and promised them that he would end the draft. According to Seymour's biographer, the governor at this time was not speaking to the rioters, who were engaged elsewhere, but to a crowd that largely looked to him to end the disorders. Even so, it is not certain that, as Horace Greeley's hostile *New York Tribune* claimed, he used the words "my friends" in addressing the gathering. Seymour always denied that he had referred to the rioters as his friends, as, he said, he had never met one. At any rate, he called for the good people of New York to defend their city against the mob. The governor also announced that he had dispatched the state's adjutant general to Washington to urge a postponement of the draft until its legality could be determined by the courts. On the same day, he issued two proclamations declaring the city and county in a state of insurrection and warning lawbreakers that they would be vigorously prosecuted.[61]

Finally, on Wednesday, July 15, the rioting subsided when military detachments from West Point and Pennsylvania arrived in the city. The civil disorder in New York left 119 people dead and a few hundred injured, though at the time, reports circulated that more than one thousand had been killed. The casualties included both black and white citizens and also policemen and soldiers who bravely confronted the rioters. Fifty large buildings were destroyed, and others severely damaged.[62]

On August 3, Governor Seymour sent the president a long account of the disorders in the city, which he blamed mainly on opposition to the "unexpected draft" and its unfairness. He denounced the federal government for leaving New York virtually defenseless, "while the militia of the City were supporting the National cause" against Lee in Pennsylvania. However, he admitted that the public was "under great and lasting obligation" for the courage, skill, and wise counsel of the handful of U.S. military and naval personnel stationed in the city. In the end, Seymour told Lincoln, "the rioters were subdued by the exertions of the City Officials, civil and military, the people, the police and a small body, of only twelve hundred men, composed equally of the State and National forces." The governor charged that the federal government had failed to "give any substantial aid" to the restoration of order in New York.[63]

In his account to Lincoln, Seymour also took the occasion to deliver a long criticism of military conscription. He particularly questioned its legality and the unfairness of the government's allocation of draft quotas for the New York City and Brooklyn districts. The implication was clear, Seymour contended: "the inequalities" in the assignment of quotas fell "most heavily upon those districts which have been opposed to [the president's] political views." To demonstrate his point, the Democratic governor cited the low quotas for upstate New York, which consisted of Republican districts, compared with the high quotas for the two Democratic districts in Brooklyn and New York City. He "earnestly requested" that the president direct the enrolling officers to "submit to the State authorities their lists, and that an opportunity shall be given to me—, as Governor of this State . . . to look into the fairness of these proceedings." Seymour insisted that the draft was unnecessary because "large numbers" were taking advantage of the state and national bounties to volunteer for the army.[64]

Regardless, Seymour declared, "the successful execution of the conscription act depends upon the settlement, by judicial tribunals, of its constitutionality." He asked the president to suspend the draft, especially in New York, until the judiciary could rule on the act's constitutionality. "A refusal to submit it to [the judicial] test will be regarded as evidence that it wants legality and binding force." Furthermore, Seymour argued, the failure of the administration to permit the courts to review the conscription act would "naturally create" hostility toward the government and "excite citizens to disobedience." The governor confidently assured Lincoln that "the submission of the Government to the decisions of our courts" on conscription "would give it a new and stronger hold upon the public confidence; it would add new vigor to our system of Government; and it would call forth another exhibition of voluntary offerings, of men and treasure, to uphold an administration which would thus defend and respect the rights of the People." Seymour wishfully predicted, "The dissentions [*sic*] and jealousies at the North, which now, weaken our cause, would at once be healed up, and your voice would be potential [potent] in calling forth the power and force of a united people."[65]

On August 7, Lincoln responded to Seymour's appeal to suspend the draft: he refused. The president's decision to continue the draft was bolstered by Union military successes at Gettysburg and Vicksburg in early July. Furthermore, state Republican officials, who feared the consequences for raising troops and suppressing Copperheads in their states if Lincoln submitted to Seymour's demands, wanted the draft to go forward in New York. Governor Kirkwood of Iowa expressed the concern of Republican governors when he telegraphed Secretary of War Stanton on July 15, "The enforcement of the draft throughout the country depends upon its enforcement in New York City. If it can be successfully resisted there, it cannot be enforced elsewhere. For God's sake let there be no compromising or half-way measures."[66]

The president, citing the need to replace the losses sustained at Gettysburg and elsewhere, wrote Seymour, "Time is too important" to permit the draft's suspension or wait for a judicial ruling on its constitutionality. However, he conceded, "I do not object to abide a decision of the United States Supreme Court" eventually. Lincoln told the New York governor that he did not believe that a "great disparity" existed in the quotas for the state's enrollment districts. Much of the difference, he argued, could be "accounted for by the fact that so many more persons fit for soldiers, are in the city than are in the country, who have too recently arrived from other parts of the United States and from Europe." In closing, Lincoln insisted, "My purpose is to be, in my action, just and constitutional; and yet practical, in performing the important duty, with which I am charged, of maintaining the unity, and the free principles of our common country."[67]

If Lincoln thought his explanation would satisfy the governor, he was sadly mistaken. Seymour, again referring to conscription statistics for the New York districts, dispatched a voluminous report, written by New York's judge advocate general, to Washington to demonstrate "the strongest proofs of injustice if not of fraud in the enrolments of certain districts [and] a dishonest perversion of law." The state, Seymour informed the president, "has never paused in its efforts to send volunteers to the assistance of our gallant soldiers in the field. It has not only met every call heretofore made, while every other Atlantic and each New England State save Rhode Island was delinquent." He maintained that "exertions [to] organize and fill up old regiments . . . would be more successful if the draft was suspended. [Then] much better men than reluctant conscripts would join the armies."[68]

Lincoln still refused to call off the draft, though he agreed that, after the first draft of men, several New York districts would be reenrolled to remedy any injustices that had occurred. Not surprising, Seymour continued to find problems with the administration of conscription in his state.[69] However, when the draft was resumed on August 19 in New York, no resistance occurred. One day earlier, the governor issued a proclamation to New Yorkers announcing that his criticism of conscription did not justify violence against its enforcement. He warned that further riotous conduct would not be tolerated. The remedy for the wrongs of federal conscription, Seymour reminded opponents of the draft, was through the courts.[70] The fate of conscription and other war policies, he told New Yorkers as well as others, also rested with the ballot box.

In New Jersey, Joel Parker, the only other Democratic governor in the North, took a less confrontational approach to the draft than Seymour. Shaken by the rioting across the Hudson River in New York, Parker issued a proclamation on July 15 against any acts of violence and warned New Jerseyans to avoid heated political discussions and gathering in large crowds. On the same day, Parker warned Lincoln of "a deep rooted hostility" to the conscription act in his state, which could "lead to popular outbreak if . . . enforced." He did not desire at this time to discuss the constitutionality of conscription, nor, he said, was "it proper to state causes, which . . . have induced the present condition of affairs. I take things as they are." Nonetheless, Parker agreed with Seymour that the legality of conscription should be decided by the courts as soon as possible. He asked Lincoln to postpone the draft in New Jersey until he had time to raise volunteers, which he had already begun, to meet the state's projected draft quota.[71]

On July 20, Lincoln replied that if Parker "could push forward [his] volunteer regiments as fast as possible," it would lessen "the draft so much [and] may supersede it altogether." The president reminded the New Jersey governor, "It is a very delicate matter to postpone the draft in one State, because of the argument it furnishes others to have postponements also." A few days later, Lincoln, having learned that New Jersey was still behind in meeting its quota, asked Parker for "a point of time, to which we could wait, on the reason that we were not ready ourselves to proceed, and which might enable you to raise the quota of your state, in whole, or in large part, without the draft." Until then, Lincoln said, the draft must proceed toward the goal of meeting the state's quota for men. He told Parker, "If we get well through with this draft, I entertain a strong hope that any further one may never be needed"—a hope that proved wrong.[72]

The off-year elections in the fall of 1863 caused Lincoln and the Republican governors deep concern, despite dramatic battlefield successes at Gettysburg and Vicksburg and a renewed determination in the North to win the war. Still, the opposition to conscription, especially its perceived unfairness, and the unrelenting Copperhead campaign against emancipation, the suppression of the press, and arbitrary arrests could mean defeat for the Republicans in the key states of the lower North. Lincoln defused some of the Copperhead criticism by postponing further drafts until 1864. Republicans were especially anxious about Ohio and Pennsylvania, where gubernatorial elections in October could serve as a harbinger for the outcome of future contests.

In Ohio, the state Democratic convention had nominated Copperhead Clement Vallandigham for governor in a foolish act of defiance against his Republican tormentors. The "apostle of peace" was living in Canada after his arrest by Burnside and his banishment by Lincoln. Even in exile, Vallandigham inspired Ohio Democratic speakers and editors to conduct a scorched-earth campaign against Lincoln's policies and to support a platform calling for a cease-fire in the war, followed by a peace conference. Many Copperheads naively believed that an armistice and negotiations with Jefferson Davis would lead to the restoration of the Union and the Constitution as it had been.[73]

Ohio Republicans, meeting in Columbus and calling themselves the Union Party, rejected Governor David Tod as their candidate and nominated John Brough for governor. Tod expressed his wish to be renominated, but old political rivalries came back to haunt him. Tod had chaired the Democratic convention in Baltimore in 1860, which had nominated Stephen A. Douglas for president, and this still bothered prewar Republicans, many of whom had been Whigs. The governor's appointment of former Democrats, though not Copperheads, to civil and military positions also hurt his efforts to be renominated. Secretary of the Treasury Chase had appointed Treasury officials in Ohio who, as Radical Republicans, opposed the governor. Tod had become a loyal supporter of Lincoln, which did not sit well with Chase activists in the state, who were already scheming to place their champion in the White House.[74]

Although Tod had served ably in behalf of the Union, and under demanding circumstances, some Ohio Republicans believed that as governor he lacked sufficient vigilance in suppressing home-grown "traitors" and Copperheads. The state Union Party (Republican) convention nominated Brough, who had been living in Indiana for several years. Brough was a former Democrat, but he had not been active in the party since 1848. He could win the votes of all factions that supported the war, including many conservatives who opposed Lincoln's Emancipation Proclamation. Furthermore, Brough's championing of the railroads in the states, particularly the consolidation of the east-west lines, gained him some critical votes in the convention that ensured his nomination.[75]

Even though Tod was upset by his defeat in the convention, he assumed the political high ground and campaigned for Brough's election. The governor telegraphed the president that his loss in the convention could not be attributed to his "advocacy of the leading measures of [Lincoln's] Administration." "Personal considerations alone," he informed Lincoln, "were the cause of my defeat." Tod assured the president, "No man in Ohio will do more to secure the triumphant election of the [Republican] ticket than I will," a promise that he kept. Lincoln, on his part, consoled him: "I deeply regret that you were not re-nominated—not that I have ought against Mr. Brough. On the contrary, like yourself, I say, hurrah, for him."[76] The president did not forget Tod's sterling support for the war and his policies. In an ironic twist, Lincoln's first choice to replace Chase, when he resigned as secretary of the treasury in 1864, was the former Ohio governor. Tod declined the position.

The opening of the Mississippi River for western products after the fall of Vicksburg, in addition to the victory at Gettysburg, bolstered morale throughout the West and strengthened the Republican campaign in Ohio. During the summer, Governor Tod and gubernatorial candidate Brough rallied Ohioans against Confederate general John Hunt Morgan's bold invasion of the state, leading to the celebrated rebel raider's capture at New Lisbon and imprisonment in the Ohio State Penitentiary. (Morgan would later escape.) In probably the most divisive political contest in Ohio history, Republican speakers and editors carried on an unrelenting campaign against the Copperheads, condemning Vallandigham as a "traitor" and predicting that if he won in the October 13 election, civil war would erupt in the state. By the late summer, however, it was clear to Ohio Republicans that they would win the election.[77]

Still, Lincoln fretted about the outcome in Ohio and to a lesser extent in Pennsylvania. He waited throughout election night for the voter returns from Ohio. Finally, Brough telegraphed him at five o'clock the next morning that he had defeated Vallandigham by more than 100,000 votes, a victory augmented by more than

41,000 votes from troops in the field, compared with 2,388 soldiers' votes for Vallandigham. The president could not contain his joy—and relief—on receiving the news from the state. He immediately telegraphed the governor-elect, "Glory to God in the Highest, Ohio has saved the Nation."[78] On the same day, Lincoln told Secretary of the Navy Gideon Welles that he "had more anxiety in regard to the election results of yesterday" than he had in 1860, when he was chosen president. Yet he "could not believe that Vallandigham could have been the candidate of a large party, [and] received a vote that is a discredit to the country."[79]

On October 15, Lincoln also received joyous news from Senator James W. Grimes in Iowa and Governor Andrew Curtin in Pennsylvania. In Iowa, Republican candidates "swept the state overwhelmingly," Grimes happily reported. In Pennsylvania, Curtin, though sick and unable to conduct a vigorous campaign, still won reelection by about 15,000 votes over George W. Woodward, who was a more acceptable Democratic candidate than Ohio's Vallandigham. Woodward, a justice of the state supreme court, was a staunch states' rights advocate who opposed conscription and other Lincoln policies. Pennsylvania Republicans, campaigning for Curtin, unfairly but effectively characterized Woodward as a "traitor" in the mold of Vallandigham. Even in Indiana, where Copperhead strength was the greatest and no gubernatorial election occurred, Governor Morton telegraphed the president the day after the election that Union or Republican Party candidates had made important gains in county contests.[80]

In the November legislative elections in New York, Republicans captured two-thirds of the districts, dealing a blow to Governor Seymour and the Democrats. In New Jersey, Republicans made important inroads into the state's large Democratic majority.[81] In Missouri and Maryland, candidates advocating gradual emancipation, though mainly opposed to black recruitment and military intervention in civil affairs, gained control of the state legislatures. However, the Copperhead or antiwar movement, particularly in the lower North, was not dead. But for now, Lincoln's war policies, including emancipation and military conscription, were safe.

The people's commitment to the war and their support for Lincoln would be severely tested in 1864 by a stalemate on the battlefield. As the terrible war entered its fourth year, the Union governors, as before, played important roles in maintaining Union morale and encouraging perseverance to final victory. Another series of critical elections would also occur in the fall, for president, several Northern governors, a new U.S. House of Representatives, and state legislatures. These elections could determine the future for the Union and emancipation.

THE UNION TRIUMPHANT

On January 19, 1864, in Harrisburg, Governor Andrew Curtin gave his second inaugural address. Speaking on a platform with the original Declaration of Independence beside him, he admonished Pennsylvanians and others in the Union states to "subordinate all things . . . for the preservation of our national life." The governor reminded the people that Lincoln's election in 1860, "in strict conformity with the constitution and the laws, though not the cause" of secession, "was deemed the fit occasion for an organized attempt to overthrow the whole fabric of our free institutions, and plunge a nation of thirty millions into hopeless anarchy." The "grave offence" charged against Lincoln at the time, he reminded his audience, consisted only "in his avowed fidelity to the government and his determined purpose to fulfill his solemn covenant to maintain inviolate the union of the States."[1]

"Three years of bloody, wasting war, and the horrible sacrifice of a quarter of a million lives attest [to] the desperation" of the rebel leaders' "purpose to overthrow our liberties" and institutions, Curtin continued. "Our people," he exclaimed, "have been sorely tried by disasters" in the war; "but in the midst of the deepest gloom they have stood with unfaltering devotion to the great cause of our common country." God, in His "own good time," will assert "His own avenging power." Curtin abandoned any caution about proclaiming his support for emancipation. "As this war is now persisted in by the leaders of the rebellion, it has become evident that slavery and treason, the fountain stream of discord and death, must soon share a common grave," he announced. Curtin steeled Pennsylvanians against any compromise with the rebels. A compromise peace, he warned, would give the rebellion "renewed existence, and enable it to plunge us into another causeless war. In the destruction of the military power of the rebellion, is alone the hope of peace" and the preservation "of our free institutions."[2]

Governor John Brough of Ohio, in his inaugural address on January 11, expressed similar sentiments in rallying his people for a final push toward victory in the war. He reminded Buckeyes of what was at stake: the nation was "struggling for its existence—of freedom gasping for its vitality—of a good and beneficent government laboring to assert its supremacy over a rebellious and misguided portion of its people." Echoing Lincoln's opinion on the universal meaning of Union success in the war, Brough declared, "The restoration of our Government and Union will be potent in its influence, not only upon ourselves but the civilized world. It involves the question of man's capacity for self-government, [and] whether a government resting solely upon its people, and controlled by delegated powers, possesses the elements of strength and unity to protect itself and assert its sovereignty in such an emergency as a great revolution or rebellion inaugurated among a portion of its own people for its destruction."[3]

Brough gave powerful notice to Ohioans: "While this struggle continues, privations and sacrifices will continue with it." Meanwhile, he declared, "we must alleviate, as much as practicable, the sufferings and bear with fortitude the burthens imposed upon us." He specifically asked the Ohio legislature for a higher tax than Governor Tod had recommended, to aid the families of the state's "soldiers and marines." Brough also announced that the Union armies must be reinforced and increased by troops from Ohio and other states for the spring campaign. "Present events indicate very strongly that the end of the rebellion is rapidly approaching," he told his people.[4]

Like Curtin, the Ohio governor insisted that peace and the restoration of the Union could occur only with the defeat of the rebel armies. But, he said, "it does not follow that the destruction of the military power of the South" would mean "the subjugation of the people." The majority of Southerners, Brough predicted, would hail their deliverance from the rebel hierarchy. Reflecting Lincoln's policy outlined in his Proclamation of Amnesty and Reconstruction, issued one month earlier, the governor asserted, "The loyal people of the Southern States, be they few or many, can alone be entrusted with this great work of reorganization."[5]

Other Republican governors also used their inaugural addresses or annual messages to their legislatures to rally the people for the military campaigns and the sacrifices to come. Lincoln's reshuffling of the military command structure, placing U. S. Grant in overall command of the army with his headquarters in Virginia, Sherman in north Georgia, and Nathaniel P. Banks in Louisiana, received the governors' wholehearted support. Backed by the loyal people, the Union would soon triumph over the rebels, the governors confidently told their people. On January 11, Minnesota governor Henry A. Swift, who had replaced Alexander Ramsey when he was elected to the U.S. Senate in July 1863, reported to his legislature, "The rebellion already staggers, death-struck to its fall. [A] succession of glorious victories have dispelled [the earlier] gloom and banished every lingering doubt of the fast approaching result in the total overthrow of the base conspiracy against Constitutional Liberty." Governor Swift happily announced, "The delusive cry of 'Peace,' is no longer heard" in the North. "Slavery, the foul-nursing-mother of all this woe, must share the fate of her offspring [treason], and is now writhing in the throes of dissolution." After the war, Swift predicted, "the old bonds of Union will return, [as] made plain" by President Lincoln in his Proclamation of Amnesty and Reconstruction.[6]

Two days later, Stephen Miller succeeded Swift as governor. A veteran of several battles in Virginia, Miller had returned home to Minnesota in 1862 in time to participate in the mass hangings of thirty-eight Dakota Sioux warriors at Mankato after the failure of the Indian uprising. His comments on assuming office were like those of Swift, Curtin, and Brough. Miller, however, only briefly mentioned the end of slavery as one of the consequences of the war.[7] In supporting emancipation, Miller and the Republican governors, with the notable exception of those of New England, did not foresee at this time that the federal government had a constitutional duty to guarantee the civil liberties of the freed people after the war. They expected true Unionists (white people), who, they believed, had been suppressed by the rebel military arm, to be empowered and given the responsibility for determining the status of African Americans in the South.

As Union armies prepared to launch their spring 1864 offensives in the South, General in Chief Grant informed the War Department and the governors that he needed more troops. Governor Brough persuaded four other western governors to go with him to Washington and present Lincoln with a plan to obtain the men on a short-term basis. Joined by Morton of Indiana, Yates of Illinois, and new governors William M. Stone of Iowa and James T. Lewis of Wisconsin, Brough met with Lincoln and Stanton on April 21 and secured an authorization for the five western governors to provide eighty-five thousand troops to serve for one hundred days where needed "within or without" their states. The number of troops would be apportioned based on the populations of the western states, with Ohio, the most populous, providing the largest number. The governors promised to raise these troops immediately. General Grant admitted that he opposed receiving men for such a brief period of service, but, he conceded, "they might come at such a crisis as to be of vast importance."[8]

Only Ohio met and exceeded its quotas for the one hundred days' men. At least one governor, Lewis of Wisconsin, explained that he could not fulfill his quota until his regiments had received arms. Despite difficulties in finding available men to recruit and in providing arms for them, the new western troops, by garrisoning forts and protecting vulnerable railroads, released veterans for critical frontline combat in the South.[9]

The high hopes at the beginning of 1864 for an early defeat of the rebels were soon shattered. The Union armies in Virginia, northern Georgia, and the Red River valley of Louisiana during the spring and summer became mired in brutal, casualty-inflicting fighting with Confederate forces. At home, uncertainty grew, and Union governors fretted about the course of the war. On May 24, Brough, who had emerged as a leader among the governors, anxiously telegraphed

Stanton, "Have you anything cheering or consoling that you can give me [about the military situation]? . . . Do you still retain your perfect confidence in the result?" When Stanton showed Lincoln the telegram, the president answered it by citing the latest message from General Grant. The commanding general reported that the army facing General Lee above Richmond had crossed the North Anna River, saying, "Everything looks exceedingly favorable for us."[10] But as Lincoln, Brough, and other Union leaders soon found out, Union forces in Virginia under Grant failed to achieve their objectives: the destruction of Lee's army and the capture of the Confederate capital. Grant had to settle for a grueling siege of Petersburg. At the same time, General Sherman fared no better in his efforts to take Atlanta, the key to the lower South. In Louisiana, General Banks retreated after a series of battles along the Red River.

Inevitably, morale plummeted again in the North. On July 18, Lincoln issued a call for five hundred thousand additional volunteers, and at the same time, he scheduled a draft for September 5 to include areas that had not met earlier quotas.[11] The call for more troops increased skepticism in the Union states that the war could be won in 1864, if at all. With the approach of important fall elections, including those for president, Congress, and governors of Indiana, Illinois, and New York, the situation seemed dire indeed for Lincoln and the Republicans. The unpromising course of the war by midsummer had provided the Copperhead peace movement with a dramatic new lease on life, particularly in the vulnerable and all-important states of the lower North. Meeting in Baltimore in June, before the full political impact of the military campaigns had been felt, the Republicans, renamed the National Union Party, or simply the Union Party, had renominated Lincoln on a war platform that also supported a constitutional amendment abolishing slavery. The Democrats chose to delay their national convention until August 29, when, they believed, the political situation would be clearer and to their advantage.

By August, Lincoln had become the target of almost all who were despondent about the war. In his own party, many Republican leaders concluded that the Union cause and its candidates would be defeated in the fall elections if Lincoln remained as the party's standard-bearer. Although the Republican governors withheld their public criticism of the president, Yates, Morton, Austin Blair of Michigan, and the New England governors believed that Lincoln had proven incapable of providing the necessary leadership to win the war, much less the presidential election. Few were more concerned about the future of the Union and emancipation if the Copperheads prevailed in the fall elections than Governor Andrew of Massachusetts. His anxiety led him to write to Democratic Governor Seymour on August 11, asking if they could meet in New York, "and in the confidence of gentle-men," discuss whether they "might not unite to strengthen the arms of [their] National power." The cooperation of the two governors dur-ing the crisis, Andrew informed Seymour, would "help to 'conquer a peace' by the use of means [designed to] invigorate the patriotism of the people, and thus avoid many of the evils" that had naturally settled upon the country because of the long war.[12]

Seymour agreed to confer with the Massachusetts governor, but instead of meeting in New York, he made a surprise visit to Andrew's office in Boston. After introducing himself (apparently they had never met), Seymour announced, "I do not agree with all of your opinions, but I like you because you have convictions." Believing that they both had a common enemy in Secretary of State Seward, reputedly the evil genius behind the president, Seymour told Andrew, "Seward has no convictions; I cannot get along with him, so I have called to talk matters over with you." After a two-hour meeting, the two governors failed to agree on any point. According to Andrew, the principles of the "old Democracy" were too ingrained in Seymour for him to overstep party lines and cooperate with a Republican governor.[13] The same could have been said about the Massachusetts governor's commitment to his own party's principles.

Meanwhile, the National War Committee of prominent New York Republicans, mainly of the anti-Seward faction, met and decided that the only hope for the party in the fall election and the nation was to hold another convention and replace Lincoln as the party's candidate for president. The committee sent out a printed circular let-ter to about forty important eastern Republicans who, they believed,

shared their view that a new party convention should be held to
select a presidential "candidate who commands the confidence of
the country." They called for the convention to meet in Cincinnati
on September 28. Mailed on August 25, the letter apparently went to
only one governor, John Andrew. Most of the respondents favored
the call for the convention; all believed that a crisis had been reached
in the war and a change was necessary to avoid defeat. Andrew,
however, preferred to wait until after the Democratic convention in
late August to reply to the committee.[14]

The actions of the national Democratic convention at Chicago
on August 29–31 and the fall of Atlanta to Sherman on September
2, followed by the stunning successes of General Philip Sheridan's
forces in the Shenandoah Valley, created a sea change in the fortunes
of Lincoln and the Republican Party. The Democrats adopted the
Copperhead platform, pronouncing the war a failure and demanding that "immediate efforts be made for a cessation of hostilities,
with a view to an ultimate convention of states" for the restoration
of the Union. The status of slavery would be left to the states. The
Democrats nominated General McClellan for president; however, the
general repudiated the party's resolution calling for an armistice, but
not the remainder of the platform promising the restoration of the
Union "as it was." (McClellan resigned his commission on the day of
the election.) Lincoln and the Republicans, including the governors,
concluded, perhaps correctly, that Democratic success in the election
would lead to Confederate independence.[15]

On September 2, Horace Greeley and two other New York editors wrote the Republican governors and asked them three leading
questions: "1. In your judgment is the re-election of Mr. Lincoln a
probability? 2. In your judgment can your own state be carried for
Mr. Lincoln? 3. In your judgment do the interests of the Union party
and so of the Country require the substitution of another candidate
in place of Mr. Lincoln?" By the time the governors had received
the questionnaire and responded, the fall of Atlanta was known,
and most of them declared that Lincoln should not be replaced as
the party's candidate. Governor James T. Lewis of Wisconsin emphatically replied, "The interests of the Union party, the honor of the

Nation and the good of Mankind, demand that Mr. Lincoln should be sustained and re-elected."[16] Governor Yates of Illinois answered, "The substitution of another man at this late date would be disastrous to the highest degree." Other Republican governors concurred but expressed reservations about Lincoln. Governor William M. Stone of Iowa wrote that, "running on his own merits or personal popularity," Lincoln could not win, but the voters understood "the mighty issues at stake" in the election and "the disastrous consequences which would inevitably result from his defeat."[17]

Although he agreed reluctantly with the other governors that, as a matter of necessity, Lincoln should not be replaced as the Union Party candidate, Governor Andrew could not resist taking a backhanded and condescending swipe at the president in his reply to the New York editors' questionnaire: "Mr. Lincoln *ought* to lead the country. But he is lacking in the essential qualities of leadership, which is a gift of God and not a device of man. Without this, his other qualities, as an able and devoted magistrate and most estimable citizen, leave it necessary for us to make a certain allowance for a measure of success which, under the more magnetic influence of a positive man, of clear purpose and more prophetic instinct, would surely be ours." The Massachusetts governor told Greeley, "I trust that zeal and energy, however, on the part of the faithful who mean to preserve Liberty and the Government, will enable our Cause to win, irrespective . . . of the merits" of the party's candidate.[18]

Opposed by the party's governors and frightened by the Democratic war-failure platform, dissident Republicans wisely recognized the need to drop their opposition to Lincoln. The proposed Cincinnati convention never met. Andrew still worried that Lincoln, in order to win the election, would be pushed by Seward and conservatives like Henry J. Raymond, editor of the *New York Times* and chairman of the national Republican committee, "to an unworthy and disgraceful offer to compromise with the leaders of the Rebellion." To secure the support of governors Yates, Morton, and Brough, Andrew asked them to meet him in Washington, where, along with others, they would seek to "take hold" of Lincoln and "guard and protect him" against misguided leaders in the party. Although the western governors could not join the Massachusetts governor in Washington, Yates and Brough wrote supporting letters to Andrew, which he showed to Lincoln. Andrew had a "frank talk" with the president and encouraged him to stand firm behind the party platform and the Union objectives in the war.[19] Lincoln had already rejected peace talks with the Confederates that did not include the end of the rebellion and reunion. He also had refused to abandon emancipation as a war aim, regardless of its impact on the election.

Lincoln and the Republicans still feared that their now promising election prospects could be reversed. It could happen if the military successes in Georgia and Virginia were not sustained and the casualty lists continued to grow, providing the Northerners and border state people with little hope for an early end to the war. To ensure a Union victory in the election, the Republican governors, along with others, took to the stump to campaign for Lincoln and party candidates. Governor Andrew brought his considerable influence in the Northeast to bear by campaigning in New York as well as in his home state. His emphasis, however, was not only on Lincoln's merits but mainly on the disaster to the Union cause that would occur if Republicans were divided and a Copperhead government came to power in Washington.[20] The only two Democratic governors, Seymour and Parker, supported McClellan in the election, but they did not campaign on their party's Copperhead or cease-fire platform.

In the West, Governor Brough, an accomplished orator, toured Ohio, stumping for Lincoln and condemning the Chicago platform. At Circleville, Brough thundered that the Democrats in the Chicago convention had "marshaled . . . a faction of men seeking to obtain the power of the Government." This faction, he said, "aided the rebels in bringing this rebellion upon us, and . . . now want to get control of affairs so as to wind it up to suit themselves and their traitor Democratic brethren in the South." "This is not the time for" complaints about the conduct of the war, Brough declared; "that time will come by and by, when criticism may be indulged in without injury to our country's cause. [Now] we must stand by the platform that pledges unwavering support of the Union, until the rebellion is crushed, or the rebels willingly lay down their arms" and yield "obedience to the laws and the Constitution." Furthermore, he announced, the Union Party and Lincoln would end slavery, while the Democrats would permit the evil institution to continue to plague the nation and its political system.[21]

Like other Republican speakers in the campaign, Brough ended with an appeal to patriotism and to honor the troops' sacrifices for the Union. He exclaimed that the voters owed it to the soldiers in the field to cast their ballots for Lincoln in the election. "Great God!" he shouted, "are you going to suffer the word to them that they have to submit to giving up all they have struggled so hard to gain, to go back and leave their comrades in the soil! [sic] Are you going to say to them that they must surrender all the conquests of four years for the manufacture of a batch of political conspirators?" Brough's compelling speech was published in pamphlet form and circulated throughout the state and elsewhere; Lincoln received a copy.[22]

As most political observers believed, state elections in Indiana, Ohio, and Pennsylvania in October would go far toward determining the outcome of the presidential contest in November—and thus the ultimate course of the war. Of these states, only Indiana was holding an election for governor. There, Governor Morton campaigned not only to win a second term in office but also to regain control of the legislature for the Union Party from the Democrats and eliminate the Copperhead threat in the state. Furthermore, the results in the three lower Northern states would influence the important November state elections in New York, where Republican Reuben Fenton was challenging incumbent Seymour, the bête noire of eastern Republicans and the administration in Washington. In Illinois, Republican Richard J. Oglesby, a war hero and a political friend of Lincoln's, was running against Congressman James C. Robinson, a Democrat with strong Copperhead leanings. In Missouri, Thomas Fletcher, another Union war hero, hoped to become the first Republican governor of a border slave state.

The October election in Indiana created the most concern for Lincoln. There, Morton repeatedly appealed to Lincoln for help against the Democrats. The governor told the president that the Indiana

Copperheads "intend[ed] to fight with a desperation and bitterness unparalleled in the history of political warfare." He warned, "If they succeed the influence of the State will be turned against your Administration and the War policy with all the malignity they can muster."[23] Morton went to Washington and, along with the Indiana Republican delegation in Congress, asked Lincoln to suspend the draft. Otherwise, he feared, the Copperheads would win the election and Indiana would "practically" end its military aid to the federal government. The president refused to postpone the draft, explaining to Morton, "It is better that we both should be beaten than that the forces in front of the enemy should be weakened on account of the absence of these men."[24]

Lincoln, however, agreed to ask, not order, General Sherman, who commanded most of the Indianans in the Union army, if he could "safely" let his Indiana troops, "or any part of them, go home and vote at the State election." In his letter to Sherman, he impressed on the general the importance of the Indiana election, informing him that "the loss of it to the friends of the Government would go far towards losing the whole Union cause." The furloughed soldiers, the president said, "need not remain for the Presidential election." He reminded Sherman that Indiana was the only important state whose troops could not vote in the field.[25] Sherman was sufficiently impressed by the need. He granted furloughs to sick and wounded Indiana soldiers so they could go home and vote. Although they did not make a difference in the Indiana election, which was won handily by Morton and the Republicans, several thousand furloughed Hoosiers voted, a large majority casting ballots for the Union Party candidates.[26]

Republicans also won Ohio and Pennsylvania in October, though the margin of victory was close in the Keystone State. In the November elections, Lincoln captured all but three states, Delaware, New Jersey, and Kentucky. In the last two states, Governors Joel Parker and Thomas Bramlette campaigned for McClellan. (Bramlette was a conservative Unionist, not a Democrat.) Fenton defeated Seymour for governor of New York, which must have greatly pleased Lincoln. In Missouri, Fletcher won the gubernatorial election, bringing to power the radical Unionist faction, which would soon abolish slavery in the state and politically proscribe Confederate sympathizers. Oglesby and the Republicans fairly easily regained complete control of Lincoln's home state. An overwhelming majority of soldiers in the nineteen states that permitted voting in the field cast ballots for Union Party candidates, but only in New York and Connecticut did they likely determine the outcome. Lincoln probably would have won without the votes of the soldiers.

The election of 1864 willed that slavery would soon end everywhere in the United States, and it also meant that there would be no compromise on reunion. Governor William Buckingham of Connecticut, as did other Republican governors, exulted in the victory at the polls. He wrote to Lincoln, "Permit me to congratulate the nation & the friends of human liberty everywhere that our true able & ever faithful President has been reelected to the highest position on earth."[27] On January 31, 1865, Congress approved a resolution initiating the proposed antislavery amendment to the Constitution, and Lincoln sent it to the states for ratification. The Union governors lobbied their legislatures for its quick approval, which in most cases soon occurred. Even the border state governors, including Bramlette of Kentucky, urged their General Assemblies to ratify the charter of freedom. However, both the Kentucky and Delaware legislatures rejected it. The New Jersey state senate defeated ratification in that state, the only Northern state to do so before the Thirteenth Amendment became a part of the Constitution in December 1865. Governor Parker, a supporter of the war whose bid for a U.S. Senate seat had been blocked by the Copperheads in his party, apparently remained on the sidelines in the debate on the amendment.[28]

General Lee's surrender at Appomattox on April 9, 1865, and the impending end of all rebel resistance sparked wild celebrations throughout the Union states. But a few days later, the celebrations turned to shock and profound sorrow. The assassination of Abraham Lincoln produced a wave of anger and grief. Along the route of the funeral train that carried the martyred president home to Springfield, hundreds of thousands of people, including African Americans, turned out to pay their deep respects. Thousands of mourners viewed Lincoln's body in the major cities. Each governor along the train's circuitous route met the cortege when it entered his state and escorted it to his capital and then on to the next state.

In the numerous eulogies to the fallen president, many political leaders who had often denounced and ridiculed Lincoln now praised his sterling qualities, some even admitting that they had been mistaken all along about him. Governor Bramlette, at a large memorial service in Louisville on April 18, frankly acknowledged that Lincoln "was right and we were wrong" about him.[29] No Union governor experienced such an extraordinary reversal of opinion than Governor John A. Andrew of Massachusetts, who eight months earlier had criticized Lincoln as "lacking in the essential qualities of leadership." In reporting the president's assassination to his legislature, Andrew expounded on Lincoln's remarkable qualities and his contribution to American history. Lincoln, the governor wrote, "had the rare gift of discerning and setting aside whatever is extraneous and accidental [incidental?], and of simplifying an inquiry or an argument by just discriminations. The purpose of his mind waited for the instruction of his deliberate judgment; and he was never ashamed to hesitate until he was sure that he was intelligently informed." Andrew further declared that Lincoln, though "not greatly gifted in what is called the intuition of reason, was nevertheless of so honest an intellect that by the processes of methodical reasoning he was often led so directly to his result that he occasionally seemed to rise into that peculiar sphere which we assign to those . . . who are natural leaders."[30]

Andrew told the Massachusetts legislature that it would be "challenging human history to produce the name of a ruler more just, unselfish, or unresentful than Abraham Lincoln." At the same time, he said, it would be premature "for us to assert how far [Lincoln] led the American People. The unfolding of events in the history we are yet to enact will alone determine the limits of such influence. It is enough for his immortal glory that he faithfully represented the people, their confidence in democratic government, their constancy in the hour of adversity, and their magnanimity in the hour of triumph." Finally, Andrew declared, Lincoln "proclaimed liberty to three million of American slaves, and prepared the way for Universal Emancipation."[31]

The other governors, who also had contributed to the preservation of the Union and its founding principles, probably did not read Andrew's inspiring assessment of the martyred president's qualities and leadership. If they had, they would have agreed with him.

Abraham Lincoln recognized from the beginning of the Civil War that he must have the assistance of the governors to succeed. He understood the need to respect the governors' traditional authority and that of the states in the federal system of government under the Constitution. The fact was that almost all of the western and Northern governors affiliated with Lincoln's Republican or Union Party, and they facilitated support for his war policies, which ultimately included emancipation. Even the border state governors, who had been former Whigs like Lincoln, and the important Democratic governors Horatio Seymour of New York and Joel Parker of New Jersey, though they opposed emancipation and other Lincoln policies, backed the Union military cause. The Republican governors especially played a leading role in rallying their people for the war, organizing state regiments for the Union army, and providing aid and comfort to the troops in the field. The western governors (those in today's Midwest) were often ahead of the president during the first months of the war in mobilizing their states to suppress the rebellion. During periods of gloom in 1862 and 1864, the Republican governors contributed significantly to maintaining home-front morale and fulfilling Lincoln's call for troops to replace battlefield losses. They also kept the president informed about political conditions in their states and regions, though, as in the case of Governor Morton of Indiana, they often tended to exaggerate the strength and purposes of the Democratic opposition.

At no time did the governors prove more important in providing Lincoln with the support that he needed than at the Altoona conference on September 24, 1862. Occurring at a critical time in the war and two days after Lincoln issued his preliminary Emancipation Proclamation, the Altoona meeting of about half of the governors endorsed Lincoln's actions, despite Governor Andrew's argument for a presidential proclamation freeing all slaves, including those in the Union border states. The governors, in their written address to the president, which was later printed, circulated, and signed by most of the state executives, approved Lincoln's suspension of the writ of habeas corpus, and they also called for more troops to suppress the Southern insurrection. In order not to undermine the war effort, the governors did not express their concerns about General McClellan's military leadership in their address, nor did they demand the reorganization of the president's cabinet that the Radical Republicans wanted.

In effect, the governors at Altoona and in a subsequent meeting with the president endorsed Lincoln's leadership in the war. Their support cushioned the political setbacks that the Republicans soon experienced in the crucial fall 1862 elections. The Democrats, seizing on the growing war weariness in the North and the opposition to Lincoln's antislavery and habeas corpus proclamations, swept to victories in state elections in the lower North and won the governorships of New York and New Jersey. The Republican governors, however, managed to retain control of their states for the duration of the war, though this was problematic in Indiana. The Union cause was at its greatest risk in early 1863, when Lincoln and Congress were forced to adopt military conscription. Lincoln's wise handling of Governor Horatio Seymour's efforts to obstruct federal conscription in New York preserved that state's important role in the war. Although the Republican governors were troubled by the political fallout from the $300 commutation exemption in the conscription act, as well as the federal administration of the draft in their states, they cooperated in the act's enforcement.

The tide turned for the Union and the war party after Gettysburg and Vicksburg in July 1863. Republican victories in gubernatorial elections in Ohio and Pennsylvania in the fall encouraged Lincoln, the governors, and Unionists everywhere to believe that the war would soon end with the military campaigns of 1864. The Republican governors rallied their people for the sacrifices still needed to win. However, when casualties mounted during the spring and summer and a military stalemate occurred, demoralization resulted and strong opposition to the war and to Lincoln's leadership and policies again developed. During the late summer, a northeastern Republican attempt to replace Lincoln as the party's presidential candidate threatened the Union cause as well the party's success in the fall elections. At this critical juncture in the campaign, the Republican governors, in responding to a questionnaire from Horace Greeley and two other New York editors, came out in support of Lincoln, which provided an important counterweight to the anti-Lincoln movement in the party. In the end, General Sherman's occupation of Atlanta and other Union military successes undercut the Democratic peace platform and the effort of dissident Republicans to replace Lincoln as the party's standard-bearer. The Republicans not only won the presidential election but also regained the governorship of New York and easily won in Indiana, a state where the Copperheads had flourished. The radical Union Party in Missouri placed a Republican in the governor's office, and in January, the state abolished slavery in its constitution.

The election of 1864 also willed the abolition of slavery in all of the United States and foretold an uncompromised end to the Southern rebellion. Lincoln signed the congressionally initiated Thirteenth Amendment, which was not required of him, and sent it out to the states for ratification in early 1865. The removal of the awful blemish of slavery from the American republic and the preservation of the Union owed a great deal to the cooperation that Lincoln received from the governors in the war. Unfortunately, Abraham Lincoln did not live to lead the reunited nation through its difficult adjustment to peace and freedom.

ACKNOWLEDGMENTS

My study of Abraham Lincoln, extending over a period of more than twenty-five years, has been aided by many people. Colleagues and students in the North Carolina State University Department of History have been a source of inspiration and support. Lincoln aficionados and scholars have provided information and encouragement in my study of this American icon. A special word of thanks goes to Michael Burlingame and John David Smith for their cheerful and important aid in my research and writing. Alexander J. De Grand, a colleague for many years and a member of the "Dinosaur Diners," read the manuscript and made many useful suggestions.

The librarians at North Carolina State University and at numerous other institutions have extended an unselfish hand to me in my research. I would be remiss if I did not mention the following curators of photographs who have provided digital images of the governors for this book: Jonathan Eaker, Prints and Photographs Division, Library of Congress; Anna Cook, Massachusetts Historical Society; Lily Birkhimer, Ohio State Historical Society; and Nicole Joniec, the Library Company of Philadelphia.

I am especially appreciative of the encouragement that Sylvia Frank Rodrigue of the Concise Lincoln Library has given to me regarding this study. Her coeditors, Richard W. Etulain and Sara Vaughn Gabbard, carefully read the manuscript and provided important suggestions for its improvements.

Finally, Betty Glenn Harris, my wife of more than fifty years, though not a historian, has always assisted in bringing my research and writing to fruition. I owe her a great deal.

APPENDIX: UNION GOVERNORS
DURING THE CIVIL WAR

California

John G. Downey, Democrat, January 14, 1860–January 10, 1862
Leland Stanford, Republican, January 10, 1862–December 10, 1863
Frederick Lowe, Republican, December 10, 1863–December 5, 1867

Connecticut

William A. Buckingham, Republican, May 5, 1858–May 2, 1866

Delaware

William Burton, Democrat, January 18, 1859–January 20, 1863
William Cannon, Unionist, January 20, 1863–March 1, 1865
Gove Salisbury, Democrat, March 1, 1865–January 17, 1871

Illinois

Richard Yates, Republican, January 14, 1861–January 16, 1865
Richard J. Oglesby, Republican, January 16, 1865–January 11, 1869

Indiana

Oliver P. Morton, Republican, January 16, 1861–January 23, 1867

Iowa

Samuel J. Kirkwood, Republican, January 11, 1860–January 14, 1864
William M. Stone, Republican, January 14, 1864–January 16, 1868

Kansas

Charles Robinson, Republican, February 9, 1861–January 12, 1863
Thomas Carney, Republican, January 12, 1863–January 9, 1865
Samuel S. Crawford, Republican, January 9, 1865–November 4, 1868

Kentucky

Beriah Magoffin, Democrat, August 30, 1859–August 18, 1862
James F. Robinson, Unionist, August 18, 1862–September 1, 1863
Thomas E. Bramlette, Unionist, September 1, 1863–September 3, 1867

Maine

Israel Washburn, Republican, January 2, 1861–January 7, 1863
Abner Coburn, Republican, January 7, 1863–January 6, 1864
Samuel Cony, Republican, January 6, 1864–January 2, 1867

Maryland

Thomas H. Hicks, American (Unionist), January 13, 1858–January 8, 1862
Augustus W. Bradford, Unionist, January 8, 1862–January 10, 1866

Massachusetts

John A. Andrew, Republican, January 3, 1861–January 4, 1866

Michigan

Austin Blair, Republican, January 2, 1861–January 3, 1865
Henry Crapo, Republican, January 3, 1865–January 6, 1869

Minnesota

Alexander Ramsey, Republican, January 2, 1860–July 10, 1863
Henry A. Swift, Republican, July 10, 1863–January 11, 1864
Stephen A. Miller, Republican, January 11, 1864–January 8, 1866

Missouri

Claiborne F. Jackson, Democrat, January 3, 1861–July 25, 1861
Hamilton Gamble, Unionist, July 31, 1861–January 31, 1864
Willard P. Hall, Unionist, January 31, 1864–January 2, 1865
Thomas Fletcher, Republican, January 2, 1865–January 12, 1869

Nevada (admitted as a state in 1864)

Henry Blasdel, Republican, December 5, 1864–January 2, 1871

New Hampshire

Ichabod Goodwin, Republican, June 2, 1859–June 6, 1861
Nathaniel S. Berry, Republican, June 6, 1861–June 3, 1863
Joseph H. Gilmore, Republican, June 3, 1863–June 8, 1865

New Jersey

Charles S. Olden, Union Democrat, January 17, 1860–January 20, 1863
Joel Parker, Democrat, January 20, 1863–January 16, 1866

New York

Edwin D. Morgan, Republican, January 1, 1859–December 31, 1862
Horatio Seymour, Democrat, January 1, 1863–December 31, 1864
Reuben Fenton, Republican, January 1, 1865–December 31, 1868

Ohio

William Dennison, Republican, January 9, 1860–January 13, 1862
David Tod, Union Party, January 14, 1862–January 10, 1864
John Brough, Republican, January 11, 1864–August 29, 1865

Oregon

John Whiteaker, Democrat, March 3, 1859–September 10, 1862
Addison Gibbs, Republican, September 10, 1862–September 13, 1866

Pennsylvania

Andrew G. Curtin, Republican, January 15, 1861–January 15, 1867

Rhode Island

William Sprague, Republican, May 29, 1860–March 3, 1863
William Cozzens, Union Democrat, March 3, 1863–May 26, 1863
James Y. Smith, Republican, May 26, 1863–May 29, 1866

Vermont

Erastus Fairbanks, Republican, October 12, 1860–October 11, 1861
Frederick Holbrook, Republican, October 11, 1861–October 3, 1863
James Gregory Smith, Republican, October 9, 1863–October 13, 1865

West Virginia (admitted as a state in 1863)

Arthur I. Boreman, Unionist, June 20, 1863–February 26, 1869

Wisconsin

Alexander W. Randall, Republican, January 4, 1858–January 6, 1862
Louis P. Harvey, Republican, January 6, 1862–April 19, 1862
Edward Salomon, Republican, April 19, 1862–January 4, 1864
James T. Lewis, Republican, January 4, 1864–January 1, 1866

NOTES

Introduction

1. Edmund Wilson, *Patriotic Gore: Studies in the Literature of the American Civil War* (New York: Oxford University Press, 1962), xvii–xviii.
2. Morton Keller, *Affairs of State: Public Life in Late Nineteenth Century America* (Cambridge: Harvard University Press, 1977), 20.

1. The Secession Crisis

1. Edward McPherson, *The Political History of the United States of America, during the Great Rebellion* (Washington, DC: Philp & Solomons, 1865), 41–42; Robert W. Johanssen, *The Frontier, the Union, and Stephen A. Douglas* (Urbana: University of Illinois Press, 1989), 69.
2. Henry Greenleaf Pearson, *The Life of John A. Andrew, Governor of Massachusetts, 1861–1865* (Boston: Houghton, Mifflin and Company, 1904), 1:248–49.
3. Ibid., Speech of Governor Andrew, at New York, September 5, 1861, *Rebellion Record: A Diary of American Events, with Documents, Narratives, Illustrative Incidents, Poetry, Etc.*, ed. Frank Moore (1862; New York: G. P. Putnam, 1977), 3:66–67; William B. Hesseltine, *Lincoln and the War Governors* (1948; Gloucester, MA: Peter Smith, 1972), 124–25.
4. Dan Elbert Clark, *Samuel Jordan Kirkwood of Iowa* (Iowa City: State Historical Society of Iowa, 1917), 224–25.
5. Stephen Engle, *All the President's Statesmen: Northern Governors and the American Civil War*, Frank L. Klement Lectures: Alternative Views of the Sectional Conflict (Milwaukee: Marquette University Press, 2006), 41n37.
6. Pearson, *John A. Andrew*, 1:116.
7. Clark, *Samuel Kirkwood*, 174–75.
8. Ibid., 177–78.
9. Abraham Lincoln (hereafter cited as AL) to William Kellogg, December 11, 1860; AL to Lyman Trumbull, December 10, 1860, in *The Collected Works of Abraham Lincoln*, ed. Roy P. Basler, (New Brunswick, NJ: Rutgers University Press, 1953), 4:149–50; entry for February 9, 1861, *The Diary of Orville Hickman Browning*, ed. Theodore Calvin Pease and James G. Randall (Springfield: Illinois State Library, 1925), 1:453 (hereafter cited as *Browning Diary*), regarding Lincoln's opposition to the Peace Conference.
10. Inaugural Address of Governor Curtin, January 15, 1861, in William H. Egle, *Life and Times of Andrew Gregg Curtin* (Philadelphia: Thompson Publishing Co., 1896), 118–20.

11. Ibid., 120–21.
12. William Gillette, *Jersey Blue: Civil War Politics in New Jersey, 1854–1865* (New Brunswick, NJ: Rutgers University Press, 1994), 116, 119.
13. William E. Parrish, *History of Missouri*, vol. 3, *1860 to 1875* (Columbia: University of Missouri Press, 1973), 3–4.
14. John Niven, *Connecticut for the Union: The Role of the State in the Civil War* (New Haven, CT: Yale University Press, 1965), 36–37; Russell Mc-Clintock, *Lincoln and the Decision for War: The Northern Response to Secession* (Chapel Hill: University of North Carolina Press, 2008), 170–80; David M. Potter, *The Impending Crisis, 1848–1861*, comp. and ed. Don E. Fehrenbacher (New York: Harper & Row, 1976), 546–47.
15. William A. Buckingham to AL, December 28, 1860, Papers of Abraham Lincoln, Manuscript Division, Library of Congress, Washington, DC (hereafter cited as Lincoln Papers). Available at http://memory.loc.gov /ammen/alhtml/alhome.html/.
16. Richard H. Abbott, *Ohio's War Governors* (Columbus: Ohio State University Press for the Ohio Historical Society, 1962), 10.
17. Emma Lou Thornbrough, *Indiana in the Civil War Era, 1850–1880* (Indianapolis: Indiana Historical Bureau and Indiana Historical Society, 1965), 101; Kenneth M. Stampp, *Indiana Politics during the Civil War* (1949; Bloomington: Indiana University Press, 1978), 68–70.
18. William C. Harris, *Lincoln and the Border States: Preserving the Union* (Lawrence: University Press of Kansas, 2011), 36.
19. AL, First Inaugural Address—Final Text, March 4, 1861, *Collected Works*, 4:265–66.
20. Ibid., 262–64.
21. Ibid., 270–71.
22. Edwin D. Morgan to AL, March 5, 1861, Lincoln Papers.
23. Paul Revere Frothingham, *Edward Everett: Orator and Statesman* (Boston: Houghton Mifflin, 1925), 415.

2. The Call to Arms

1. Harris, *Lincoln and the Border States*, 39.
2. William A. Buckingham to Simon Cameron, April 15, 1861; O. P. Morton to AL, April 15, 1861; Alexander W. Randall to Cameron, April 15, 1861; William Dennison to AL, April 15, 1861; Richard Yates et al. to AL, April 17, 1861, in *The War of the Rebellion: A Compilation of the Official Records of the Union and Confederates Armies* (Washington, DC: Government Printing Office, 1880–1901), ser. 3, vol. 1, 70, 72–75, 80–81 (hereafter cited as *OR* with series and volume designations).
3. Alexander Ramsey to Simon Cameron, April 14, 1861; Samuel J. Kirkwood to Cameron, April 16, 1861, *OR*, ser. 3, vol. 1, 67, 74–75; Clark, *Samuel Kirkwood*, 180.

4. McClintock, *Lincoln and the Decision for War*, 265; AL to Charles S. Olden, May 4, 1861, *Collected Works*, 4:355.

5. Israel Washburn Jr. to Simon Cameron, April 15, 1861; John A. Andrew to Adjutant General Lorenzo Thomas, April 15, 1861; Irvin McDowell to John A. Andrew, April 15, 1861, *OR*, ser. 3, vol. 1, 71.

6. Nelson D. Lankford, *Cry Havoc! The Crooked Road to Civil War, 1861* (New York: Viking Press, 2007), 210–16.

7. Pearson, *John A. Andrew*, 1:203–7, 215.

8. Oliver P. Morton to Simon Cameron, April 24, 1861, *OR*, ser. 3, vol. 1, 108.

9. Richard Yates to Simon Cameron, April 25, 1861, *OR*, ser. 3, vol. 1, 113.

10. William Dennison to Simon Cameron, April 22, 1861; Andrew Curtin to AL, April 23, 1861; Charles Robinson to Simon Cameron, April 25, 1861, *OR*, ser. 3, vol. 1, 101, 105, 112.

11. Russell F. Weigley, *A Great Civil War: A Military and Political History, 1861–1865* (Bloomington: Indiana University Press, 2000), 56–57; AL, Proclamation Calling for 42,034 Volunteers, May 3, 1861; Message to Congress in Special Session, July 4, 1861, *Collected Works*, 4:353–54, 429.

12. Edwin D. Morgan to Simon Cameron, April 24, 1861, *OR*, ser. 3, vol. 1, 108.

13. Samuel J. Kirkwood to John E. Wool, May 6, 1861, *OR*, ser. 3, vol. 1, 163.

14. Ibid.

15. Bryce D. Benedict, *Jayhawkers: The Civil War Brigade of James Henry Lane* (Norman: University of Oklahoma Press, 2009), 30–31.

16. Abbott, *Ohio's War Governors*, 12; Pearson, *John A. Andrew*, 1:222–23; Clark, *Samuel Kirkwood*, 203; Thornbrough, *Indiana in the Civil War Era*, 107, 164–65.

17. Alexander W. Randall to AL, May 6, 1861, *OR*, ser. 3, vol. 1, 167–70; Thomas J. McCormack, ed., *Memoirs of Gustave Koerner, 1809–1896* (Cedar Rapids, Iowa: Torch Press, 1909), 2:139–40.

18. John Bigelow, *Retrospections of an Active Life* (New York: Baker and Taylor, 1909), 1:350; McCormack, *Memoirs of Koerner*, 2:139–40.

19. Bigelow, *Retrospectives of An Active Life*, 1:350.

20. Ibid., 1:350–51.

21. Alexander W. Randall to AL, May 6, 1861, *OR*, ser. 3, vol. 1, 167.

22. Ibid., 168.

23. Ibid., 168–69.

24. AL, Message to Congress in Special Session, July 4, 1861, *Collected Works*, 4:428.

25. Memorial from W. Dennison, Richard Yates, and O. P. Morton, May 24, 1861, *OR*, ser. 1, vol. 52, pt. 1, 146–47.

26. Jack Northrup, "Gov. Richard Yates and Pres. Lincoln," *Lincoln Herald* 70 (1968): 196.

27. General Winfield Scott for Simon Cameron, Remarks on a Memorial Signed by Their Excellencies the Governors of Ohio, Illinois, and Indiana, May 29, 1861, *OR*, ser. 1, vol. 52, pt. 1, 147–48.

28. Ibid.

29. William Dudley Foulke, *Life of Oliver P. Morton, Including His Important Speeches* (Indianapolis: Bowen-Merrill Co., 1899), 1:143.

30. Oliver P. Morton to AL, September 20, 21, 26, 1861, Lincoln Papers.

31. AL to Oliver P. Morton, September 29, 1861, *Collected Works*, 4:541–42.

32. Ibid., 541.

33. Lowell H. Harrison, *The Civil War in Kentucky* (Lexington: University Press of Kentucky, 1975), 21–23.

34. AL, Message to Congress in Special Session, July 4, 1861, *Collected Works*, 4:431–32.

35. Fred Albert Shannon, *The Organization and Administration of the Union Army, 1861–1865* (1928; repr., Gloucester, MA: Peter Smith, 1965), 1:46–47; Weigley, *Great Civil War*, 64–65.

36. Shannon, *Organization of the Union Army*, 1:46–47.

37. Samuel J. Kirkwood to AL, December 4, 1861, Henry Warren Lathrop, *The Life and Times of Samuel J. Kirkwood, Iowa's Civil War Governor* (Des Moines: Librarian of the State Historical Society of Iowa, 1893), 177. See ibid. 178 for his complaint to Senator Grimes.

38. Oliver P. Morton to AL, July 31, 1861, Lincoln Papers.

39. Oliver P. Morton to AL, January 15, 1863, ibid.

40. Andrew G. Curtin to John A. Wright, June 25, 1861, ibid.

41. AL to Richard Yates and William Butler, April 10, 1862, *Collected Works*, 5:186, 186n.

42. Andrew G. Curtin to AL, August 21, 1861, *OR*, ser. 3, vol. 1, 439–41.

43. John H. Reed and A. G. Browne Jr. to John A. Andrew, September 6, 1861, ibid., 813.

44. Ibid., 813–14.

45. Ibid., 814.

46. General Orders, No. 71, War Department, September 5, 1861, ibid.

47. Andrew G. Curtin to Thomas A. Scott, September 13, 1861, ibid., 510.

48. AL, Draft of Order Authorizing Benjamin F. Butler to Raise a Volunteer Force, September 10, 1861, *Collected Works*, 4:515.

49. AL, To New England Governors, September 11, 1861, ibid., 4:518–519n; John A. Andrew to Simon Cameron, September 11, 1861, *OR*, ser. 3, vol. 1, 498–99.

50. Pearson, *John A. Andrew*, 1:290–91; Dwight Foster to B. C. Sargeant, October 23, 1861; John A. Andrew to B. C. Sargeant, October 23, 1861, *OR*, ser. 3, vol. 1, 833–34.

51. Benjamin F. Butler to John A. Andrew, October 25, 1861; Andrew to Butler, October 26, 1861, *OR*, ser. 3, vol. 1, 835–36.

52. George C. Strong to A. G. Browne Jr., December 18, 1861, ibid., 846. The correspondence between Governor Andrew and General Butler, ultimately involving Washington officials, can be found in ibid., 652–55, 831–65.

53. Benjamin F. Butler, to Adjutant General [Lorenzo Thomas], November 18, 1861, ibid., 653–55.

54. AL to John M. Schofield, May 27, 1863, *Collected Works*, 6:234.

55. Pearson, *John A. Andrew*, 1:297–98; John T. Morse Jr., *Memoir of Colonel Henry Lee: With Selections from His Writings and Speeches* (Boston: Little, Brown, and Company, 1905), 74–75.

56. Ibid.

57. John A. Andrew to Lorenzo Thomas, December 27, 1861, *OR*, ser. 3, vol. 1, 851–52.

58. John A. Andrew to Charles Sumner and Henry Wilson, December 21, 1861, ibid., 864–65.

59. Charles Sumner to John A. Andrew, January 10, 1862, ibid., 865.

60. John A. Andrew to AL, January 11, 1862, ibid., 862–63.

61. Pearson, *John A. Andrew*, 1:306–7.

62. Ibid., 1:308–11.

3. The War Becomes Long

1. Shannon, *Organization of the Union Army*, 1:47.

2. David Herbert Donald, Jean Harvey Baker, and Michael F. Holt, *The Civil War and Reconstruction* (New York: W. W. Norton and Co., 2001), 235.

3. Shannon, *Organization of the Union Army*, 1:47–48.

4. Phillip Shaw Paludan, *"A People's Contest": The Union and Civil War, 1861–1865* (New York: Harper & Row, 1988), 18.

5. Thornbrough, *Indiana in the Civil War Era*, 174.

6. Ibid., 169, 175; Foulke, *Oliver Morton*, 1:165–66.

7. Foulke, *Oliver Morton*, 1:166; Richard Yates and Catharine Yates Pickering, *Richard Yates: Civil War Governor*, ed. John H. Krenkel (Danville, IL: Interstate Printers & Publishers, 1966), 169; Richard N. Current, *The History of Wisconsin*, vol. 2, *The Civil War Era, 1848–1873* (Madison: State Historical Society of Wisconsin, 1976), 310; F. Morley to Lorenzo Thomas, May 19, 1862, *OR*, ser. 3, vol. 2, 45.

8. W. K. Strong to AL, April 30, 1862, *OR*, ser. 3, vol. 2, 23; Current, *History of Wisconsin*, 2:310–11.

9. Foulke, *Oliver Morton*, 1:166.

10. Weigley, *Great Civil War*, 127–28.

11. E.g., Edwin M. Stanton to the "Governor of Maine," May 25, 1862, *OR*, ser. 3, vol. 2, 70.

12. Alexander Ramsey to Edwin M. Stanton, May 21, 1862; Nathaniel S. Berry to Stanton, May 21, 1862, ibid., 61–62.

13. Edwin D. Morgan to Edwin M. Stanton, May 21, 1862, ibid., 62. (This letter was sent before the War Department's formal call for troops.)
14. James M. McPherson, *Battle Cry of Freedom: The Civil War Era* (New York: Oxford University Press, 1988), 487–88.
15. Oliver P. Morton to Edwin M. Stanton, June 25, 1862, Lincoln Papers.
16. AL to William H. Seward, June 28, 1862, *Collected Works*, 5:291–92.
17. William H. Seward to Edwin D. Morgan and Thurlow Weed, June 28, 1862; Seward to Edwin M. Stanton, June 30, 1862, *OR*, ser. 3, vol. 2, 181–82; *Collected Works*, 5:294n.
18. Edwin M. Stanton to William H. Seward, June 30, 1862, *OR*, ser. 3, vol. 2, 182; McPherson, *Battle Cry of Freedom*, 491.
19. AL, Call for 300,000 Volunteers, July 1, 1862, *Collected Works*, 5:296–97; David Tod to Edwin M. Stanton, July 1, 1862, *OR*, ser. 3, vol. 2, 196.
20. C. P. Buckingham to Edwin M. Stanton, July 5, 7, 1862; Andrew G. Curtin to Stanton, July 5, 1862; John W. Finnell to Stanton, July 3, 1862, *OR*, ser. 3, vol. 2, 203, 205, 208.
21. John A. Andrew to Edwin M. Stanton, July 3, 1862; Charles S. Olden to AL, July 3, 1862; Andrew G. Curtin to AL, July 4, 1862; Samuel J. Kirkwood to AL, July 5, 1862, ibid., 202, 205, 206.
22. Israel Washburn Jr. to Edwin M. Stanton, July 3, 1862; AL to Washburn, July 3, 1862 (a similar letter was sent to all of the governors), ibid., 200–1.
23. Clark, *Samuel Kirkwood*, 230–31; William Schouler to C. P. Buckingham, July 8, 1862; Edward Salomon to AL, July 28, 1862; James F. Wilson to AL, July 28, 1862; Oscar Malmros to AL, July 28, 1862; Israel Washburn Jr. to AL, July 28, 1862, *OR*, ser. 3, vol. 2, 212, 265–66, 268, 270.
24. Jennifer L. Weber, *Copperheads: The Rise and Fall of Lincoln's Opponents in the North* (New York: Oxford University Press, 2006), 47; Frank L. Klement, *The Limits of Dissent: Clement L. Vallandigham and the Civil War* (1970; repr., New York: Fordham University Press, 1998), 99–101.
25. William A. Richardson to AL, August 30, 1862, Lincoln Papers.
26. Stampp, *Indiana Politics*, 118–19.
27. Pearson, *John A. Andrew*, 1:11–12,
28. Ibid., 1:26.
29. Richard Yates to Abraham Lincoln, July 11, 1862, Lincoln Papers.
30. James W. Geary, *We Need Men: The Union Draft and the Civil War* (DeKalb: Northern Illinois University Press, 1991). Chapter 3 has an excellent account of the militia bill.
31. Harris, *Lincoln and the Border States*, 184–86.
32. Entry for July 1, 1862, *Browning Diary*, 1:555; Remarks to Deputation of Western Gentlemen, August 4, 1862, *Collected Works*, 5:356–57.
33. Geary, *We Need Men*, 22–29; Weigley, *Great Civil War*, 233.

34. AL, Speech at Pittsburgh, February 15, 1861, *Collected Works*, 4:214.

35. Edwin M. Stanton, General Orders, No. 94, August 4, 1862, *OR*, ser. 3, vol. 2, 291–92; Weigley, *Great Civil War*, 233.

36. AL, To Union Governors, July 28, 1862, *Collected Works*, 5:347.

37. William A. Buckingham to AL, July 28, 1862, *OR*, ser. 3, vol. 2, 265.

38. James F. Wilson to Edwin M. Stanton, July 28, 1862; Edward Salomon to AL, July 28, 1862, ibid., 265–66, 270; Shannon, *Organization of the Union Army*, 288–89.

39. Edwin M. Stanton, General Orders, No. 94, August 4, 1862, *OR*, ser. 3, vol. 2, 291–92; Weigley, *Great Civil War*, 233.

40. Garret Davis, John B. Huston, and Richard A. Buckner to AL, September 6, 1862, Lincoln Papers.

41. Ibid.

42. AL to Horace Greeley, August 22, 1862, *Collected Works*, 5:388–89, 389n.

43. AL, Reply to Emancipation Memorial Presented by Chicago Christians of All Denominations, September 13, 1862, ibid., 5:419–20.

44. Ibid., 5:419, 423–25.

45. Andrew Curtin to AL, September 12, 1862, Lincoln Papers.

46. Weigley, *Great Civil War*, 146.

47. AL to Andrew G. Curtin, September 11, 1862, *Collected Works*, 5:414–15.

48. AL to Andrew G. Curtin, September 12, 1862, ibid., 5:417.

49. *Collected Works*, 5:417n

50. Andrew G. Curtin to AL, September 14, 1862, Lincoln Papers.

51. Report of New-York City National War Committee to AL, September 9, 1862, ibid.

52. Resolution of the National War Committee of the Citizens of New-York, September 5, 1862, ibid.; Pearson, *John A. Andrew*, 2:49n.

53. Entry for September 10, 1862, *The Salmon P. Chase Papers*, vol. 1, *Journals, 1829–1872*, ed. John Niven (Kent, OH: Kent State University Press, 1993), 378 (hereafter cited as *Chase Journals*); Hesseltine, *Lincoln and the War Governors*, 251–53.

54. Entry for September 12, 1862, *Chase Journals*, 382.

55. Harrison, *Civil War in Kentucky*, 41–42, 43; Lew Wallace, *An Autobiography* (New York: Harper and Brothers, 1906), 2:598.

56. Richard W. Thompson to AL, August 18, 1862; Jeremiah T. Boyle to AL, August 31, September 7, 1862; James Harlan, et al., to AL, September 11, 1862, Lincoln Papers; Abbott, *Ohio's War Governors*, 29.

57. Foulke, *Oliver Morton*, 1:189–91; E. B. Long with Barbara Long, *The Civil War Day by Day: An Almanac, 1861–1865* (Garden City, NY: Doubleday & Co., 1971), 264–65.

58. Harris, *Lincoln and the Border States*, 199.

59. Hamilton R. Gamble to AL, September 9, 1862, Lincoln Papers.

4. The Altoona Conference

1. Hesseltine, *Lincoln and the War Governors*, 354.
2. Egle, *Andrew Curtin*, 308.
3. Ibid.; Austin Blair, "The Conference of Loyal Governors at Altoona, Pennsylvania, in 1862," Austin Blair Papers, Bentley Historical Library, Ann Arbor, Michigan. The Bentley Historical Library has graciously provided me with a typed copy of the Michigan governor's reminiscences of the conference, which were written years after the meeting.
4. Pearson, *John A. Andrew*, 2:43, 45.
5. Ibid., 2:48, quoting Andrew.
6. Samuel G. Buckingham, *The Life of William A. Buckingham: The War Governor of Connecticut* (Springfield, MA: W. F. Adams Company, 1894), 261–62.
7. Ibid.
8. Richard Yates to AL, July 11, 1862, Lincoln Papers; Mark E. Neely Jr., *Abraham Lincoln Encyclopedia* (New York: McGraw-Hill, 1982), 341.
9. Clark, *Samuel Kirkwood*, 225; Foulke, *Oliver Morton*, 1:207.
10. Alexander Ramsey to AL, September 6, 1862, Lincoln Papers.
11. John Pope to Henry W. Halleck, September 16, 1862; Pope to Henry H. Sibley, September 28, 1862, *OR*, ser. 1, vol. 13, 642, 686.
12. David Tod to Edwin M. Stanton, September 9, 1862; Stanton to Tod, September 9, 1862, *OR*, ser. 2, vol. 4, 499; AL to Stanton, September 20, 1862; AL to Henry W. Halleck, October 5, 1862, *Collected Works*, 5:432 and n, 449 and n.
13. Kenneth Carley, *The Dakota War of 1862* (St. Paul: Minnesota Historical Society, 1976), 1 and n, 70–72.
14. David A. Nichols, *Lincoln and the Indians: Civil War Policy and Politics* (Columbia: University of Missouri Press, 1978), 117–18.
15. Nichols, *Lincoln and the Indians*, 121; Alvin M. Josephy Jr., *The Civil War in the American West* (New York: Alfred A. Knopf, 1991), 138.
16. Nichols, *Lincoln and the Indians*, 141.
17. Edward Salomon to Edwin M. Stanton, September 2, 5, 1862, *OR*, ser. 3, vol. 2, 508–9.
18. Edwin M. Stanton to Edward Salomon, September 5, 1862, ibid., 518.
19. Edward Salomon to Edwin M. Stanton, September 6, 1862, ibid., 522–23.
20. Samuel J. Kirkwood to Edwin M. Stanton, September 8, 1862, *OR*, ser. 1, vol. 13, 620; Lathrop, *Samuel J. Kirkwood*, 171–72.
21. Hamilton R. Gamble to Montgomery Blair, September 24, 1862, Lincoln Papers; William E. Parrish, *Turbulent Partnership: Missouri and the Union, 1861–1865* (Columbia: University of Missouri Press, 1963), 135.

22. James A. Rawley, "Lincoln and Governor Morgan," *Abraham Lincoln Quarterly* 6 (March 1951): 289.

23. Clark, *Samuel Kirkwood*, 248; Pearson, *John A. Andrew*, 2:50.

24. Josiah G. Holland, *The Life of Abraham Lincoln* (Springfield, MA: Gurdon Bill, 1866), 394–95.

25. Samuel J. Kirkwood, "The Loyal Governors at Altoona in 1862," *Iowa Historical Record* (1891–93): 211–12; Austin Blair, "The Conference of Loyal Governors at Altoona, Pennsylvania, in 1862," Blair Papers. Kirkwood and Blair, writing years later, provided the only accounts by the governors. Though Blair arrived too late to participate in the discussions, he was informed of the discussions by the governors and approved the address at the end of the conference.

26. *Washington National Intelligencer*, September 27, 1862; Pearson, *John A. Andrew*, 2:51–52.

27. "Address of Loyal Governors to the President, Adopted at a Meeting of Governors of Loyal States, Held to Take Measures for the More Active Support of the Government, at Altoona, Pa., on the 24th Day of September, 1862," *OR*, ser. 3, vol. 2, 583.

28. Pearson, *John A. Andrew*, 2:51.

29. John A. Andrew to "Dear A," September 22, 1862, in Albert G. Browne, *Sketch of the Official Life of John A. Andrew, as Governor of Massachusetts* (New York: Hurd and Houghton, 1868), 74.

30. Andrew G. Curtin to Alexander K. McClure, February 16, 1892, in Alexander K. McClure, *Abraham Lincoln & Men of War-Times* (1892; repr., Lincoln: University of Nebraska Press, 1997), 272n.

31. Clark, *Samuel Kirkwood*, 249; Northrup, "Yates and Lincoln," 202; Kirkwood, "Loyal Governors at Altoona," 211–12.

32. "Address of the Loyal Governors to the President," 583–84.

33. Proclamation Suspending the Writ of Habeas Corpus, September 24, 1862, *Collected Works*, 5:436–37.

34. Blair, "Conference of Loyal Governors at Altoona"; entries for September 26, 27, 1862, *Chase Journals*, 403.

35. James G. Randall, *Lincoln, the President: Springfield to Gettysburg* (New York: Dodd, Mead, 1955), 230–31.

36. Entry for September 26, 1862, *Diary of Gideon Welles: Secretary of the Navy under Lincoln and Johnson* (Boston: Houghton Mifflin, 1911), 1:153 (hereafter cited as *Welles Diary*).

37. Blair, "Conference of Loyal Governors at Altoona."

38. AL, Reply to Delegation of Loyal Governors, September 26, 1862, *Collected Works*, 5:441, as reported in the *New York Tribune*, September 29, 1862.

39. Kirkwood, "Loyal Governors at Altoona," 213.

40. Ibid., 214.

41. Blair, "Conference of Loyal Governors at Altoona."

42. Clark, *Samuel Kirkwood*, 352.

43. Entry for September 27, 1862, *Welles Diary*, 1:153.

44. Entry for September 30, 1862, ibid., 1:156.

45. James A. Rawley, *Edwin D. Morgan, 1811–1883: Merchant in Politics* (New York: Columbia University Press, 1955), 181.

46. Address to the President, September 30, 1862, Andrew Johnson Papers, Manuscript Division, Library of Congress, Washington, DC (microfilm); Parrish, *Turbulent Partnership*, 135.

47. *Boston Herald*, October 3, 1862; *Washington National Intelligencer*, September 27, October 2, 1862.

48. William B. Hesseltine and Hazel C. Wolf, "The Altoona Conference and the Emancipation Proclamation," *Pennsylvania Magazine of History and Biography* 71 (July 1947): 205. The first Hartford Convention was the secret meeting of delegates, chosen by five New England legislatures, who met at the Connecticut capital and adopted resolutions designed to interpose their states' authority against President James Madison and federal enactments supporting the War of 1812. Andrew Jackson's decisive victory over the British at New Orleans in early 1815 created a new spirit of American nationalism and discredited the Hartford Convention as disloyal.

49. Michael Burlingame, ed., *Dispatches from Lincoln's White House: The Anonymous Civil War Journalism of Presidential Secretary William O. Stoddard* (Lincoln: University of Nebraska Press, 2002), 108.

50. Pearson, *John A. Andrew*, 2:56–58.

51. Blair, "Conference of Loyal Governors at Altoona."

52. Geary, *We Need Men*, 47–48.

53. Blair, "Conference of Loyal Governors at Altoona."

54. For the fall 1862 election results, see Weber, *Copperheads*, 65–69; and James M. McPherson, *Ordeal by Fire: The Civil War and Reconstruction* (1982; repr., New York: McGraw-Hill, 2002), 319–20.

55. Blair, "Conference of Loyal Governors at Altoona."

56. McClure, *Lincoln & Men of War-Times*, 270.

57. John G. Nicolay and John Hay, *Abraham Lincoln: A History* (New York: Century Co., 1890), 6:167.

58. Pearson, *John A. Andrew*, 2:53n.

59. The New Jersey governor apparently was not related to the Harvard professor by the same name.

5. Governor Seymour and the Copperhead Threat

1. Allan Nevins, *The War for the Union: War Becomes Revolution, 1862–1863* (New York: Charles Scribner's Sons, 1960), 2:307–8.

2. Weber, *Copperheads*, 64, 67.

3. Foulke, *Oliver Morton*, 1:208–9; Nevins, *War for the Union*, 2:318; Stampp, *Indiana Politics*, 152–53.

4. Oliver P. Morton to AL, October 21, 1862, *OR*, ser. 1, vol. 16, pt. 2, 634.

5. Richard Yates and Oliver P. Morton to AL, October 25, 1862, ibid., 642.

6. Morton's complete October 27, 1862, letter to Lincoln can be found in Foulke, *Oliver Morton*, 1:208–11.

7. Ibid., 209.

8. Ibid., 210.

9. Richard L. Kiper, *Major General John Alexander McClernand: Politician in Uniform* (Kent, OH: Kent State University Press, 1999), 135–36.

10. AL to John A. McClernand, October 20, 1862; Edwin M. Stanton, order of October 21, 1862, *Collected Works*, 5:468, 469n; Foulke, *Oliver Morton*, 1:211–12.

11. Foulke, *Oliver Morton*, 1:210–11.

12. Ibid., 211–12.

13. Kiper, *John McClernand*, 141–42; John A. McClernand to AL, December 12, 1862, *OR*, ser. 1, vol. 17, pt. 2, 401.

14. John A. McClernand to AL, November 10, 1862, Lincoln Papers.

15. U. S. Grant to Henry W. Halleck, November 10, 1862; Halleck to Grant, November 11, December 18, 1862, *OR*, ser. 1, vol. 17, 469; Kiper, *John McClernand*, 146.

16. Henry W. Halleck to U. S. Grant, December 18, 1862, *OR*, ser. 1, vol. 17, 476; John A. McClernand to AL, January 7, 1863, Lincoln Papers.

17. John A. McClernand to AL, February 16, 1863, Lincoln Papers.

18. Richard Yates, Ozias M. Hatch, and Jesse K. Dubois to AL, August 6, 1863, ibid.

19. John A. McClernand to AL, September 28, October 9, 1863, January 14, 1864, ibid.; AL to McClernand, August 12, 1863, *Collected Works*, 6:383, 384n; Kiper, *John McClernand*, 291–92.

20. Nevin, *Connecticut for the Union*, 307–8.

21. Arthur Charles Cole, *The Era of the Civil War, 1848–1870*, with a new introduction by John Y. Simon (1919; repr., Urbana: University of Illinois Press, 1987), 197.

22. Abbott, *Ohio's War Governors*, 26.

23. Arnold M. Shankman, *The Pennsylvania Antiwar Movement, 1861–1865* (Rutherford, NJ: Fairleigh Dickinson University Press, 1980), 101.

24. Gillette, *Jersey Blue*, 203.

25. Pearson, *John A. Andrew*, 2:55, 60.

26. Current, *History of Wisconsin*, 2:405.

27. Josephy, *Civil War in the American West*, 238, 265.

28. Stewart Mitchell, *Horatio Seymour of New York* (Cambridge, MA: Harvard University Press, 1938), 267–68.

29. Allen C. Guelzo, *Lincoln's Emancipation Proclamation: The End of Slavery in America* (New York: Simon & Schuster, 2004), 187.

30. Abbott, *Ohio's War Governors*, 26–27; Edwin M. Stanton to David Tod, January 9, 1863; Tod to Stanton, May 27, 1863, *OR*, ser. 3, vol. 3, 8, 229.

31. Oliver P. Morton to Edwin M. Stanton, January 3, 1863, *OR*, ser. 1, vol. 20, pt. 2, 297.

32. Oliver P. Morton to AL, January 31, 1863, Lincoln Papers; AL to Morton, February 1, 1863, *Collected Works*, 6:87–88.

33. Oliver P. Morton to AL, February 9, 1863, Lincoln Papers.

34. Ibid.

35. Stampp, *Indiana Politics*, 168–69, 175.

36. Ibid., 176–78; Thornbrough, *Indiana in the Civil War Era*, 186–87.

37. Weigley, *Great Civil War*, 214; Weber, *Copperheads*, 80.

38. Cole, *Era of the Civil War*, 298–99.

39. Ibid., 300–8; Weber, *Copperheads*, 81–82.

40. Cole, *Era of the Civil War*, 302, 306.

41. Samuel J. Kirkwood to Edwin M. Stanton, March 13, 1863, *OR*, ser. 3, vol. 3, 66–68.

42. Clark, *Samuel Kirkwood*, 264–70, 274.

43. Frank L. Klement, *The Limits of Dissent: Clement L. Vallandigham & the Civil War* (Lexington: University Press of Kentucky, 1970), 49.

44. Oliver P. Morton to AL, May 30, 1863, Lincoln Papers.

45. Henry W. Halleck to Ambrose Burnside, May 20, 1863, *OR*, ser. 2, vol. 5, 664.

46. AL to Ambrose Burnside, May 29, 1863, *Collected Works*, 6:237 and n.

47. Eugene Converse Murdock, *Patriotism Limited, 1862–1865: The Civil War Draft and the Bounty System* (Kent, OH: Kent State University Press, 1967), 2, 9–10.

48. Oliver P. Morton to AL, March 6, 1863, Lincoln Papers.

49. Ibid.

50. AL, To the Senate and House of Representatives, June 8, 1864, *Collected Works*, 7:380 and n.

51. Harris, *Lincoln and the Border States*, 228, 236–40.

52. Abbott, *Ohio's War Governors*, 27; Hesseltine, *Lincoln and the War Governors*, 288–89.

53. Clark, *Samuel Kirkwood*, 294.

54. Mitchell, *Horatio Seymour*, 289–90; Klement, *Limits of Dissent*, 134–36.

55. Klement, *Limits of Dissent*, 135.

56. AL to Horatio Seymour, March 23, 1863, *Collected Works*, 6:145.

57. Ibid., 6:145–46.
58. Nicolay and Hay, *Abraham Lincoln*, 7:12–13.
59. Horatio Seymour to AL, April 14, 1863, Lincoln Papers.
60. Nicolay and Hay, *Abraham Lincoln*, 7:17; Mitchell, *Horatio Seymour*, 305–6; Adrian Cook, *The Armies of the Streets: The New York City Draft Riots of 1863* (Lexington: University Press of Kentucky, 1974), 53.
61. Mitchell, *Horatio Seymour*, 327–328; Cook, *Armies of the Streets*, 104–6; Nicolay and Hay, *Abraham Lincoln*, 7:23.
62. Cook, *Armies of the Streets*, 194–95; Samantha Jane Gaul, "New York Draft Riots," in *Encyclopedia of the American Civil War*, ed. David Heidler and Jeanne Heidler (Santa Barbara, CA: ABC-Clio, 2000), 3:1415.
63. Horatio Seymour to AL, August 3, 1863, Lincoln Papers.
64. Ibid.
65. Ibid.
66. Samuel J. Kirkwood to Edwin M. Stanton, July 15, 1863, *OR*, ser. 3, vol. 3, 494.
67. AL to Horatio Seymour, August 7, 1863, *Collected Works*, 6:369–70.
68. Horatio Seymour to AL, August 8, 1863, Lincoln Papers.
69. AL to Horatio Seymour, August 11, 1863, *Collected Works*, 6:381–82; Seymour to AL, August 21, 1863, Lincoln Papers.
70. Nicolay and Hay, *Abraham Lincoln*, 7:37.
71. Gillette, *Jersey Blue*, 243; Joel Parker to AL, July 15, 1863, Lincoln Papers.
72. AL to Joel Parker, July 20, 25, 1863, *Collected Works*, 6:347–48.
73. Klement, *Limits of Dissent*, 184–86.
74. Samuel Galloway to AL, August 22, 1863, Lincoln Papers.
75. Abbott, *Ohio's War Governors*, 36–37; Daniel J. Ryan, *Lincoln and Ohio* (1923; repr., Dover, OH: One Hundredth Press, 2008), 170; Samuel Galloway to AL, August 22, 1863, Lincoln Papers.
76. David Tod to AL, June 18, 1863, *OR*, ser. 3, vol. 3, 380; AL to Tod, June 18, 1863, *Collected Works*, 6:287.
77. Ryan, *Lincoln and Ohio*, 170; Samuel Galloway to AL, August 22, 1863, Lincoln Papers.
78. Ryan, *Lincoln and Ohio*, 172; Abbott, *Ohio's War Governors*, 40.
79. Entry for October 14, 1863, *Welles Diary*, 1:470.
80. AL to James W. Grimes, October 15, 1863, *Collected Works*, 6:515 and n; Shankman, *Pennsylvania Antiwar Movement*, 123–31, 151.
81. McPherson, *Battle Cry of Freedom*, 687–88; Gillette, *Jersey Blue*, 246.

6. The Union Triumphant

1. Egle, *Andrew Curtin*, 169–70.
2. Ibid., 170–71.

3. *Inaugural Address of John Brough, Governor of Ohio, Delivered before the Senate and House of Representatives, Jan. 11, 1864* (Columbus, OH: Richard Nivens, State Printer, 1864), 306–7, 309–10.

4. Ibid., 307–8.

5. Ibid., 311.

6. *Annual Message of Governor Swift to the Legislature of Minnesota, Delivered January 11, 1864* (St. Paul: Frederick Driscoll, State Printer, 1864), 31–33.

7. *Inaugural Address of Gov. Miller, Jan. 13, 1864* (n.p., n.d.), 10–11.

8. Abbott, *Ohio's War Governors*, 41; AL to Edwin M. Stanton, April 21, 1864; AL to Stanton, April 23, 1864, *Collected Works*, 7:308, 312 and n.

9. Geary, *We Need Men*, 133; James T. Lewis to AL, May 24, 1864, Lincoln Papers.

10. John Brough to Edwin M. Stanton, May 24, 1864; AL to Brough, May 24, 1864, *OR*, ser. 3, vol. 4, 405.

11. Geary, *We Need Men*, 152.

12. John A. Andrew to Horatio Seymour, August 11, 1864, in Pearson, *John A. Andrew*, 2:157.

13. Pearson, *John A. Andrew*, 2:158 and n; Morse, *Memoir of Colonel Henry Lee*, 237.

14. The *New York Sun* on June 30, 1889, printed the circular and a collection of letters in response to it.

15. William C. Harris, *Lincoln's Last Months* (Cambridge, MA: Belknap Press of Harvard University Press, 2004), 21, 24–25.

16. James T. Lewis to Horace Greeley, Theodore Tilton, and Parke Godwin, September 7, 1864, Lincoln Papers.

17. Michael Burlingame, *Abraham Lincoln: A Life* (Baltimore: Johns Hopkins University Press, 2008), 2:665–66.

18. John A. Andrew to Horace Greeley, September 3, 1864, in Pearson, *John A. Andrew*, 2:162–63; Burlingame, *Abraham Lincoln*, 2:665.

19. Pearson, *John A. Andrew*, 2:168–71.

20. Ibid., 2:173.

21. *The Defenders of the Country and Its Enemies. The Chicago Platform Dissected, Speech of Governor Brough, Delivered at Circleville, Ohio, Sept. 3* (Cincinnati: Gazette Company, 1864), 5, 16. A copy can be found in Lincoln Papers.

22. Ibid.

23. Oliver P. Morton to AL, August 9, 1864, Lincoln Papers.

24. Foulke, *Oliver Morton*, 1:366.

25. AL to William T. Sherman, September 19, 1864, *Collected Works*, 8:11, 12n.

26. McPherson, *Battle Cry of Freedom*, 804–5.

27. William A. Buckingham to AL, November 17, 1864, Lincoln Papers.

28. Harris, *Lincoln and the Border States*, 263; Gillette, *Jersey Blue*, 298, 302–3.

29. Lowell H. Harrison, *Lincoln of Kentucky* (Lexington: University Press of Kentucky, 2000), 11.

30. Browne, *Life of John A. Andrew*, 162–63.

31. Ibid., 163–64.

BIBLIOGRAPHICAL ESSAY

The student of the Civil War will be surprised to learn that there is no modern study of the relationship of Lincoln and the Union governors. William B. Hesseltine's *Lincoln and the War Governors* (1948, 1972), though dated, has generally been accepted as the standard account of the subject. Hesseltine's book reflected the consensus view of mid-twentieth-century historians that the Civil War president, in addition to beating back a radical challenge in his party to his leadership, by late 1862 had taken the measure of the Union governors and had found them inferior and unable to meet the unified demands of the war. By the time the governors met on September 24, 1862, at Altoona, Pennsylvania, in an important conference on the war, Lincoln, according to Hesseltine, had triumphed over them and was now the complete master of Union war policies, including the raising of troops and emancipation.

Historians have generally followed Hesseltine's view of the Union governors. They have virtually ignored the Altoona conference, which was followed by the governors' meeting with the president in Washington. Allan Nevins, in *War Becomes Revolution* (1960), volume 2 of his magisterial history, *The War for the Union*, provides a brief account of the Altoona conference, which he concludes was "an innocuous farce" (239–40). James G. Randall, in volume 2 of another classic study, *Lincoln the President: Springfield to Gettysburg* (1945), asserts that the president by the time of the Altoona conference "had clipped the gubernatorial wings," and the governors had "nothing to do but to endorse the President's policy" (231). Several decades later, Eric Foner, in his prize-winning *The Fiery Trial: Abraham Lincoln and American Slavery* (2010), devotes only two sentences to the conference and ignores the role of the governors in emancipation (230). Allen C. Guelzo, in his fine book, *Lincoln's Emancipation Proclamation: The End of Slavery in America* (2004), mentions the Altoona conference in passing (160). Russell Weigley, in *A Great Civil War: A Military and Political History, 1861–1865* (2000), gives little attention to the activities of the governors in the war and writes that the Altoona meeting "proved to be perfectly timed not to embarrass the President but to be obliged to praise his proclamation" (191–92).

Except for accounts of Lincoln's call for troops early in the war, general histories of the Civil War have neglected the governors' role in the war and their relationship to Lincoln. On the other hand, several state histories of the war, biographies, and articles describe the activities of specific governors (for example, John A. Andrew of Massachusetts and Oliver P. Morton of Indiana), their interactions with Lincoln, and the prosecution of the war. For a good understanding of the tensions and complexities that the governors faced at home, the Civil War student and reader should consult the following superb state studies: Kenneth M. Stampp, *Indiana Politics during the Civil War* (1949, 1978); John Nevin, *Connecticut for the Union: The Role of the State in the Civil War* (1965); and William Gillette, *Jersey Blue: Civil War Politics in New Jersey, 1854–1865* (1995). Richard H. Abbott's *Ohio's War Governors* (1962) is an informative brief account of this state's three governors during the Civil War.

Robert H. Jones's *The Civil War in the Northwest* (1960) is a fine study that focuses on the Indian conflict in today's upper Midwest, which spilled over into the Great Plains. Also, Alvin M. Josephy Jr.'s *The Civil War in the American West* (1991) is a well-written account that should be consulted by anyone interested in California, Oregon, Nevada, and the western territories during the war. The relationship of Lincoln with the governors of Maryland, Missouri, and Kentucky figures prominently in my book *Lincoln and the Border States: Preserving the Union* (2011). For Lincoln during the Civil War, Michael Burlingame's two-volume biography of the sixteenth president, *Abraham Lincoln: A Life* (2008), is indispensable.

These old biographies of five Union governors contain a wealth of materials and important information: William Dudley Foulke, *Life of Oliver P. Morton, Including His Important Speeches* (1889); William H. Egle, *Life and Times of Andrew Gregg Curtin* (1896); Henry Greenleaf Pearson, *The Life of John A. Andrew, Governor of Massachusetts, 1861–1865* (1904); Henry Warren Lathrop, *The Life and Times of Samuel J. Kirkwood, Iowa's Civil War Governor* (1893); and Stewart Mitchell, *Horatio Seymour of New York* (1938).

The main documentary sources on Lincoln and the governors are *The Collected Works of Lincoln* (1953–1955, 1974, 1990); the Papers of Abraham Lincoln, Manuscript Division, Library of Congress, easily accessible on the Internet through the auspices of the Library of Congress and the Lincoln Studies Center, Knox College; and *The War of the Rebellion: A Compilation of the Official Records of the Union and Confederate Armies* (1880–1901). The incoming letters and documents in the Lincoln Papers provide an underused source of information on the governors' perspectives on the war, political problems and conflict, and Lincoln's policies. The official messages of the governors reveal important insights on their activities during the war. The above sources, as well as others cited in the endnotes, have been invaluable in my research for the book.

In a lecture at Marquette University in 2006, historian Stephen Engle expressed the need for a reevaluation of the governors' role in the war. Engle pointed out that Civil War historians "have all but ignored the fact that northern governors believed that federalism and consequently states' rights did not die with secession" (5). Indeed, neither Lincoln nor the Union people thought that this was the case. Lincoln was keenly aware of the need to gain the governors' support, and in turn the people's, on important issues relating to the war. Distinguished Lincoln scholar Don Fehrenbacher notes in *Lincoln in Text and Context* (1987), "Lincoln's policy-making reflected the orthodox conception of the United States as a relatively decentralized federation in which the state governments played the most active and versatile part" (118). However, Fehrenbacher does not describe the influence of the governors on the president's decisions and policies.

A history of Lincoln's interaction with the governors and the role of the state executives in the war provides a revealing lens for viewing the Civil War and the reasons for the Union victory. Professor Engle is working on a comprehensive account of the Union governors during the war. When published, the book will be a welcome addition to the historical literature of the Civil War. In conclusion, it is probably only a slight exaggeration to say that the governors were as important as the generals in the Union's and Lincoln's success in winning the war.

INDEX

Each image in the photograph gallery, which follows page 78, is indicated in this index by an italicized *g* followed by a number representing the order of the image within the gallery.

Minnesota, 21, 58, 62–63, 113. *See also* Ramsey, Alexander

Mississippi-Ohio River basin, trade curtailments feared, 22

Mississippi River, navigation and control of, 25, 82–83, 108

Mississippi River campaign, 83–85

Missouri: Confederate invasion threat, 57–58; election of 1863 in, 109; election of 1864 in, 120–21; Fletcher as governor, 1, 120–22; Gamble as governor, 58, 65, 74; Jackson as governor, 1, 10; as Union slave state, 4

Missouri-Kansas border conflict, 58

Morgan, Edwin D.: Altoona conference and address, 65–66, 74; concerns about equipment and uniforms, 19; focus of, 7; legislative approval for raising Union troops, 16; to Lincoln on first inaugural address, 14; Lincoln's call for additional troops, 44; Lincoln's visit to New York state legislature, 12; recruitment and command issue, 32; representative to Cleveland conference, 23; response to request for troops to defend Washington, D.C., 42; and secession crisis, 9; as "war minister," 3

Morgan, John H., 57, 108

Morton, Oliver P., *94*; aid to troops, 40; Altoona conference and address, 61; arrest of suspected traitors ordered by, 92; brigadier general nominations protested by, 30; conspiracies reported by, 80; criticism of Lincoln, 46; election of 1862 and, 90; election of 1863 and, 109; election of 1864 and, 120; expansion of state militia sought by, 11; funding for Indiana government and military, 93; information provided to Lincoln, 124; intervention in Kentucky urged by, 28; to Lincoln on commutation clause of Enrollment Act, 97; to Lincoln on condition

of affairs in Indiana and the North West, 91–92; to Lincoln on Copperhead threat to 1864 election, 120–21; to Lincoln on Mississippi River campaign, 84; to Lincoln on rebel invasion of Kentucky, 80–81; to Lincoln on situation in the West, 81–83; Lincoln's appreciation for dedicated leadership of, 41; and Lincoln's reelection, 118–19; and Lincoln's visit to Indiana state legislature, 12; meeting with Dennison and Yates, 26; and one hundred days' men, 114; proposed solution to western problem, 83; purchase of weapons to arm Indiana troops, 21; response to call for troops, 18; response to Lincoln's call for additional troops, 45; response to rebel invasion of Kentucky, 57; secession crisis and, 11–12; with Sherman in advance to Corinth, 40–41; to Stanton on Copperhead conspiracies, 91; to Stanton on secret societies, 43; support for using emancipation as military tool, 61; tenure as governor of Indiana, 4; as "the soldiers' governor," 39–41; view of Burnside's actions, 95; as "war minister," 3

National War Committee, New York, 55–56, 116–17

Native Americans, 58, 62–65

Nevada, admission to statehood, 4

New England Radicals, 60

New England states, 10, 17, 55–56, 82, 88–89

New Hampshire, 42

New Jersey: adoption of Copperhead resolutions by legislature of, 90; election of 1862 in, 88; election of 1863 in, 109; election of 1864 in, 121; rejection of Thirteenth Amendment, 122; and secession crisis, 10. *See also* Olden, Charles S.; Parker, Joel

William C. Harris, professor emeritus of history at North Carolina State University, is the author of eleven books on Civil War and Reconstruction topics, including four on Lincoln. His latest book, *Lincoln and the Border States: Preserving the Union*, was the cowinner of the 2012 Lincoln Prize.

CONCISE
LINCOLN
LIBRARY

This series of concise books fills a need for short studies of the life, times, and legacy of President Abraham Lincoln. Each book gives readers the opportunity to quickly achieve basic knowledge of a Lincoln-related topic. These books bring fresh perspectives to well-known topics, investigate previously overlooked subjects, and explore in greater depth topics that have not yet received book-length treatment. For a complete list of current and forthcoming titles, see www.conciselincolnlibrary.com.

Other Books in the Concise Lincoln Library

*Abraham Lincoln and
Horace Greeley*
Gregory A. Borchard

Lincoln and the Civil War
Michael Burlingame

Lincoln and the Constitution
Brian R. Dirck

*Lincoln and the
Election of 1860*
Michael S. Green

Lincoln and Reconstruction
John C. Rodrigue

Lincoln and Medicine
Glenna R. Schroeder-Lein

*Lincoln and the
U.S. Colored Troops*
John David Smith

Lincoln and Race
Richard Striner

Lincoln as Hero
Frank J. Williams

*Abraham and
Mary Lincoln*
Kenneth J. Winkle